OHIO
Ice Cream

A SCOOP OF HISTORY

Renee Casteel Cook

THE
History
PRESS

Published by The History Press
Charleston, SC
www.historypress.com

Front cover, top: Double down on Jeni's delicious flavors and house-made buttermilk waffle cones. *Jeni's Splendid Ice Creams*. *Center*: Velvet Ice Cream opens additional distribution centers and adds to their vehicle fleet for direct delivery. *Velvet Ice Cream*. *Bottom, left*: A Jersey cow up close and personal at Young's. *Young's Jersey Dairy*. *Bottom, right*: Does a double rainbow mean double sprinkles? When they're Little Ladies Sparkle Sprinkles, the answer is always yes! *Phil Navatsyk*.
Back cover, top left: Graeter's shop in Mariemont, late 1960s. *Graeter's*. *Top, right*: Each pint packed carries the story of Alice and Handel's, made fresh at each location since 1945. *Handel's Ice Cream*. *Bottom*: Ohioans happily indulge even in chillier temps; after all, at Johnson's, snow comes in the form of sprinkles. *Johnson's Real Ice Cream*.

First published 2022

Manufactured in the United States

ISBN 9781467150965

Library of Congress Control Number: 2022931375

Notice: The information in this book is true and complete to the best of our knowledge. It is offered without guarantee on the part of the author or The History Press. The author and The History Press disclaim all liability in connection with the use of this book.

The noblest art is that of making others happy.

—P.T. Barnum

———⊶∞∞∞⊷———

*This book is dedicated to the artisans—big and small, new and longstanding,
modern and traditional—who bring smiles to faces young and old,
in times good and not so good.*

Because ice cream really does make everything better.

CONTENTS

Contents

ACKNOWLEDGEMENTS

First and foremost, I'd be remiss not to start by thanking my mother, Donna, the woman who let me start my love of ice cream by choosing chocolate rather than "kid-safe" vanilla, who claims we went almost daily after preschool and certainly trekked out in the depths of many Chicago winters for my favorite treat.

Then, thank you to my husband, Jim, who similarly ventured out into more than one dark night, especially during the third trimesters of both of my pregnancies, to fetch a flavor I couldn't shake the craving for and happily helped me finish many a pint.

And, of course, to my three girls, now equally ice cream connoisseurs, though their choices sometimes surprise me, still very much veering toward eye-catching colors over particular preferences for flavor. Oh, and sprinkles—always add sprinkles.

To EACH OF THE shops featured in this book, I extend great gratitude for the time and energy you spent (especially in the craze of summer) speaking with me, sharing your story and gathering beautiful photography to represent your stunning creations.

To my editor, John, I thank you for, first and foremost, the opportunity to explore and capture the deliciousness that is Ohio's rich dairy history, as well as your fortitude in checking batch after batch of imagery. I know it made me hungry, and you were at a distinct disadvantage of not being able to taste test from a few states away. When you make it to Ohio, I'll treat.

To Tiffany, without whom I remain doubtful I would've ever had the pleasure of calling myself a capital *A* Author. Whether it was the alignment of our stars or your wisdom and willingness to take a newbie under your wing that brought us together, I continue to be in awe of the work you do, and I am so proud of what we've done together. Every time I hold a printed work in my hand and know I've contributed, either in the writing, the editing or even the indexing (ha!), it's an honor and a joy.

To Beth, who took a chance on a recovering ad agency account person, letting me break the barrier between the C-suite and the mysterious land of Creative, thank you for offering me a gateway to marry my innate passions for writing and food as I embraced both in my new home.

And lastly, to the Ohioan turned Chicagoan who graciously allowed this Chicagoan turned Ohioan to shepherd her concept through to completion, while I'm sure I took some license of my own, I hope it lives up to your idea of the storytelling and becomes a piece of our shared history.

INTRODUCTION

*I*f Ohio is the "Heart of It All," then it's no wonder that ice cream, a sweet treat close to all of our hearts, has a long and storied history here, a history of creation, development and ongoing innovation. From the ingenuity of late 1800s and early 1900s dairy farmers, mom-and-pop shops were born, evolving from roadside storefronts to front-of-the-house sales operations, with back-of-the-house (or even the basement) production facilities.

Many of these early innovators were new Americans, having emigrated from countries with rich dairy histories, such as Switzerland, Greece and Lebanon, now combining their cultural knowledge with a new and fanciful frozen trend. Determined to make a successful start in their new home, their timing coincided with a major growth in technology, allowing them to capitalize on what was once a much more limited endeavor.

How Ice Cream Came to America and How America Made Ice Cream

While ice cream didn't originate in the United States, it was widely popularized here in the early 1900s, two hundred years after originally making its debut in the French cookbook *L'Art de Faire des Glaces*, the first known book of recipes entirely dedicated to ice cream as we know it today (previous iterations, more flavored ice than cream, date back as far as Catherine de

Medici in the sixteenth century, thirteenth-century explorer Marco Polo or even ancient China three to four thousand years ago). In America, the first record of the dish being served is a letter dated from the same year as the French cookbook, in which William Black, a Virginia official and dinner guest of Maryland governor Thomas Bladen, refers to it as "a Dessert no less curious; among the Rarities of which it was Compos'ed was some fine Ice Cream which, with the Strawberries and Milk, eat most Deliciously."

While the trend grew slowly in the early colonial days, likely due in equal parts to the cost of ingredients and lack of refrigeration, mentions in cookbooks continued to increase. Irish author Hannah Glasse's 1748 work *The Art of Cookery Made Easy*, the first English-language cookbook to include a recipe for ice cream, was followed by Richard Brigg's *The New Art of Cookery*, circa 1792, which included the first ice cream recipe published in the United States.

Around the same time, many credit Thomas Jefferson as the first American to record a recipe for ice cream (one of only ten recipes surviving in his handwriting), which likely came from his French butler; Jefferson then helped popularize ice cream by serving it during his presidency.

While ice cream was a treat reserved for only the wealthiest eighteenth-century Americans, early nineteenth-century innovations saw its ubiquity grow right alongside its popularity. By 1828, New York City street vendors were hawking the treats with cries of "I scream, ice cream," the foundation for the now familiar, "I scream, you scream, we all scream for ice cream" (an actual song written in 1927). A major development came in 1843, when a Philadelphia woman by the name of Nancy Johnson patented her invention, the hand-cranked ice cream freezer. This first step in automating the ice cream–making process greatly reduced the time and effort required to make ice cream and allowed it to be more widely available. Johnson sold the patent to William G. Young, a Baltimore native, in 1848. Young improved on the ice cream freezer, though kept her name in homage, calling it the "Johnson patent ice cream freezer." Another Baltimore businessman, Jacob Fussel, had ice cream on the brain when an opportunity to take the dairy surplus from his milk delivery business and manufacture ice cream led him to build the first ice cream factory in Pennsylvania in 1851, eventually moving it back to Baltimore in 1854. Credited with the country's first wholesale production of ice cream, Fussel was deemed the "father of the ice cream industry" for having made the product accessible to the masses. Perry Brazelton, a protégé of Fussel, followed suit, opening a wholesale ice cream plant in St. Louis in 1858, followed shortly thereafter by one each in Chicago and Cincinnati.

The next major category disrupter, invented right around the same time, allowed Fussel, Brazelton and others jumping onto the proverbial ice cream wagon to meet the growing demand. German engineer Carl von Linde developed industrial refrigeration during the 1870s, eliminating the need to cut and store ice and opening up the market for home freezers, such as the Peerless and Giant models made by the Gooch Company in Cincinnati in the 1880s.

With affordable ice cream spurring massive category growth throughout the United States, innovators were busy developing everything from flavors to delivery mechanisms. Cones (more on those and their Ohio ties in a bit), bars and sandwiches were all developed as categories of novelties; the Eskimo Pie, the Klondike Bar and a lineup of Good Humor Ice Cream Suckers all came to be during the late 1910s and early 1920s. During the same period, ice cream was given "essential food" status, after the industry petitioned the government to qualify for sugar rations put in place due to World War I.

Quick on the heels of all this innovation, the category saw yet another boost from the enactment of Prohibition laws with the passing of the Volstead Act in 1920. With consumers opting for the sweet treat as an alternative to alcohol, ice cream consumption is estimated to have grown roughly 40 percent between 1920 and 1929. In fact, in order to survive the period, now-iconic alcohol producers, including both Anheuser-Busch and Yuengling, relied partially on ice cream production. As soda fountains expanded (with some even bending the rules by serving alcohol for medicinal purposes in concoctions that combined ice cream with spirits such as bourbon), further innovations in ice cream production and, most importantly, refrigeration greatly supported the spread.

It was also during this time that the continuous-process freezer was introduced, once again changing the game of mass production. The 1926 invention by Clarence Vogt offered an alternative to the once solely batch process and, some say, gave birth to the modern ice cream industry, allowing larger producers to meet growing demand while reducing prices even further. While the repeal of Prohibition and war rations on milk and sugar slightly stalled ice cream's growth, in the mid-1940s and into the early 1950s, ice cream had another major moment, with both ice cream packaged to store in home refrigerators and electric motor options for hand-crank machines once again boosting its popularity.

While the 1970s recession could've caused another downturn in the charted course of ice cream sales, the youthful culture and renewed interest in smaller pleasures buoyed the category directly into the more prosperous '80s. A complementary shift toward personality-driven brands marked the time, including now-iconic Ben & Jerry's, founded in 1978. This "super-premium" offering directed the category toward the ingredient-driven focus that dominated the 1990s, alongside growing health trends, such as nondairy alternatives. In the first two decades of the 2000s, another shift, this time toward ice cream as an entire experience, aligned with a return to ice cream's community-based roots; while soda fountains and even old-fashioned parlors aren't as common (though they offer even more authentic nostalgia), modern shops strive to serve as a gathering place, much in the way their predecessors did.

Ohio's Role at the Heart of the Ice Cream Industry

Both in the early years of growth and modern times of continued innovation, Ohio has been well positioned at the center of the ice cream industry. While the number of dairy farms has contracted in recent years, Ohio is still ranked eleventh among the states for milk production, with approximately two thousand working dairy farms still in operation. While most simply provide their products to ice cream producers, a select few have expanded their own operations to get into the ice cream business, recognizing the opportunity to bring a super-fresh product to smiling faces.

With a midwestern mentality of almost self-deprecating modesty, Ohio's legacy of hardy dedication to the land has served as the backdrop for ice cream businesses both generational and entrepreneurial. While it's impossible to cover the hundreds of shops across the state, from homemade cottage industry pop-ups to household brand names growing cross-country empires, the stories of those included in this book are representative of the wide variety of committed excellence found from rural towns to the "three C's" (Columbus, Cleveland and Cincinnati).

Whether they opened their doors for the first time during a winter so cold the locals thought they might be crazy (then fell completely crazy themselves for the delicious custardy take on ice cream) or survived a summer heat so sweltering it shut down their soft serve machine (a quick pivot to offering just vanilla kept the wheels rolling and the chocolate sauce flowing), these neighborhood icons have developed fiercely loyal followings, no matter the conditions. For midwesterners, especially Ohioans, ice cream has become so iconic that many make an evening bowl every bit as much a part of their daily diet as their morning coffee (or milk, age dependent). Freezers can be found stocked with favorite flavors for each family member, and though families may visit a shop less frequently than they eat ice cream at home, the experience is every bit as important as the product itself. In fact, multiple shop owners simply say that what they're really selling is happiness.

Through multiple wars, financial crises and, most recently, during the COVID-19 pandemic, there is an industry sentiment that economics need not apply because of the joy ice cream brings, even in difficult times. The notion that even when you don't have much, you have enough for a scoop prevails as people seek comfort both in the consumption as well as the ritual of taking one's family for a treat that will lift spirits without breaking the bank. Put simply, ice cream has become the iconic little luxury of the masses.

In 1984, to celebrate its status, President Ronald Reagan deemed July National Ice Cream Month, with the second Sunday National Ice Cream Day (also of note is Ice Cream for Breakfast Day, the first Saturday in February, created by a New York mom in the 1960s and spread globally by her grandchildren, now often tied to charitable fundraising). Since 2019, the Ohio Farm Bureau has leveraged this timing to host the annual Ohio Farm Bureau Ice Cream Battle, which saw nearly five hundred nominations and twenty-five thousand votes in just its second year. In 2021, Tom's Ice Cream Bowl, which we'll visit in a bit, took the top spot (Deersville General Store took the first win in 2019, while Michael's Ice Cream snagged 2020's vote).

Though the process of freezing a mix of milk, sugar and flavorings to make ice cream has become simpler over its history of innovation, in many aspects, the business of it has actually grown more complicated. From sourcing to safety protocols, such as pasteurizing and homogenizing, to packaging, shipping and—in the case of those with storefronts—scooping, as well as the always competitive space of marketing one's offering as different from others', maintaining and/or building a legacy in the ice cream category takes more than a sweet tooth. Ohio has long been at the forefront or, perhaps better said, the heart of the ice cream industry, with founders and families committed to serving up smiles in each and every cone and cup.

It's no wonder this legacy includes quite a few claims to fame. Let's dig in!

Chapter 1

OHIO ICE CREAM FIRSTS

*O*ften associated with the Wright Brothers, Neil Armstrong (and John Glenn), Halls of Fame for both Rock & Roll and Pro Football and the invention of not just the hamburger but also the hot dog, Ohio has a list of "firsts" that's both lengthy and varied. The state's contributions to the ice cream industry are equally impressive; it has served as the birthplace of essentials and classics from the (highly contested) ice cream cone to the banana split and the first ice cream truck. Integral to the growth of the category and foundational for future enterprises, such as the mobile food industry, these ice cream inventions should be among the top innovations credited to Ohioans.

An Iconic Cone: Then and Now

There's great debate over who created the first ice cream cone, with up to five potential claimants, all of whom were said to be inspired in some part by the 1904 World's Fair in St. Louis. As the fair is said to have had approximately fifty ice cream stands and many waffle vendors, quite a few variations of the story developed as the cone spread across the country.

First, there's New Yorker Italo Marchiony, an Italian immigrant who claimed to have begun producing cones in 1896 and was actually granted a patent in 1903. Next, Ernest A. Hamwi, a Syrian concessionaire selling zalabis, a waffle-type crisp pastry, at the fair, who rolled his product to help a neighboring ice cream vendor who had run out of dishes (possibly at the suggestion of Abe Doumar, a Lebanese immigrant working at the fair who would also enter the business afterward). Similar stories claim that Nick Kabbaz, a Syrian immigrant who would go on to be president of the St. Louis Ice Cream Cone Company, or David Avayou, a Turkish native who would later be hired by a Philadelphia, Pennsylvania department store to set up an ice cream concession, may have come up with the inspired idea.

However, also at the World's Fair were established entrepreneurs and inventive Ohio brothers Frank and Charles Menches, who had famously created America's first hamburger at the 1885 Erie County Fair. The Menches family legacy claims the pair were topping waffles baked in Parisian irons with ice cream at the 1904 event when the idea arose (perhaps to offer a lady friend a daintier way to eat the treat) to "wrap a warm waffle around a fid, a cone-shaped splicing tool for tent ropes." Once the waffle cooled, it held its shape, providing an "edible handle for eating ice cream." Upon returning home to Akron, the Menches used their Popcorn Works factory to begin producing "premium" cones, starting the Premium Ice Cream Cone and Candy Company (the duo is also credited with combining the candy-coated peanuts and popcorn originally sold under the name Gee Whiz, now known as Cracker Jack). At the height of production, company records indicate it produced sixty thousand cones per day to keep up with growing demand for the now-popular delivery mechanism. With three locations in the Akron-Canton area today, the Menches Brothers' casual dining restaurants carry on the legacy of the products created over one hundred years ago, even occasionally bringing out an antique cone machine (one of three believed to still exist; the others are housed at the local historical society and the Smithsonian Museum), which is heated over an open flame and produces twenty cones per hour.

Cone production expanded quickly through the early 1920s, reaching a record 245 million in 1924, the same year in which Carl Taylor of Cleveland was issued a patent for his invention, the cone rolling machine. Having attended the 1904 World's Fair himself while on summer break from the Ohio State University, where he studied mechanical engineering, Taylor became fascinated with both ice cream and the cone. He was determined to develop a machine to automate the process, thus reducing cost and amping up production. Taylor's patent described it as a "machine for forming thin, freshly baked wafers while still hot into cone shaped containers." Using a turntable, the machine featured multiple dies that rotated the formed cones as they cooled and hardened. It was set up next to another machine that baked the wafer batter, supplying flat wafers hot for pressing. This dynamic duo became

NORSE DAIRY SYSTEMS

http://www.norse.com/

Founded in the 1960s, Norse Dairy Systems (NDS) has grown to be the world's largest manufacturer of sugar cones. Headquartered in Columbus, the company has facilities across the Midwest and also manufactures machinery that fills ice cream cones, such as those made by Drumstick (see "Inside Scoop" for more on that company's Ohio connections). With continued improvements to the automated process, machines today are able to produce up to 150,000 rolled cones in about twenty-four hours. Notably, NDS also invented the ice cream tube, used for treats such as the Push-Up Pop. Still operating today, the company is now a division of Interbake Foods, a subsidiary of Canada-based George Weston Limited.

the basis for Taylor's Ice Cream Cone Company, which manufactured cones until the 1960s, when it was purchased by Norse Dairy Systems.

Inside Scoop: Ohio State University and the Drumstick Sundae Cone

While the Drumstick sundae cone was invented in Fort Worth, Texas, the Parker Food Science and Technology Building at the Ohio State University (OSU) in Columbus bears the last name of its creators, brothers I.C. and J.T. "Stubby," because of a meaningful origin story and long-lasting connection. In 1928, the Parker brothers reached out to food scientists at the university to help them solve a problem they encountered while packaging ice cream cones to be shipped to sellers. To prevent the cones from getting soggy when wrapped, the OSU team coated them in chocolate, subsequently moving the coating to the inside rather than the outside of the cone. Legend has it that one of the brothers' wives actually named the product, saying it resembled a fried chicken leg, or a drumstick.

While the original partnership was pro bono, descendants of the family—who relocated their Big Drum Inc. operation to Columbus in 1930 (it would later be renamed Drumstick Inc. and eventually sold to Nestlé

Just across campus from the Parker Building sits Mirror Lake, once home to the Mirror Lake Creamery. Dale Johnson carved the 1,500-pound limestone ice cream cone, which he says is a double dip of cherry. While a 2018 remodel to the Mirror Lake Eatery means the dining spot no longer serves up scoops, the menu retains an offering of milkshakes, from classic vanilla and chocolate to specials such as strawberry cheesecake. *Dale Craig Johnson.*

in the 1990s)—including Stubby's son Tom, would become benefactors of OSU. Opened in 2000 and completed in 2002, the Parker building, which houses a retail dairy store, was named to honor the family's ongoing support of the school.

SPLIT DECISION: HAZARD'S RESTAURANT AND THE WILMINGTON BANANA SPLIT FESTIVAL

Hosted the Second Weekend of June in Denver Williams Park
https://bananasplitfestival.com/

Another ice cream icon, another highly contested debate over its origins. Cities big and small, including Boston, Chicago and Davenport, Iowa, all share stories of its invention in the first years of the 1900s (bananas had become widely available in the United States in the late 1800s), making timing truly everything.

But whether the true originator was Ernest R. Hazard of Wilmington, Ohio, who claims to have invented the banana split as part of a 1907 competition to create a new dish for his namesake restaurant, or David Strickler of Latrobe,

Pennsylvania, who supposedly came up with the idea three years earlier at the Tassell Pharmacy, where he worked (and would later buy, renaming it Strickler's Drug Store), there's no doubt that the city of Wilmington laid claim first, hosting its annual Banana Split Festival every summer since 1995 (Latrobe's "Banana Split Celebration" began in 2013). However the split got its start, it's now known for its size: three scoops of ice cream nestled between a split banana (in a dish made specifically for the long dessert, often referred to as a "boat"), topped with chocolate, strawberry and pineapple sauces and a mountain of whipped cream sprinkled with crushed nuts and maraschino cherries (Strickler's variation is said to have originally added marshmallow).

A sure sign of summer for the small town of just over twelve thousand, the Wilmington Banana Split Festival features as its centerpiece a "Make Your Own Banana Split" booth, offering even more inventive toppings and going through more than seven hundred gallons of vanilla, chocolate and strawberry ice cream (formerly provided by Gibson's Goodies ice cream parlor, a town fixture from 1947 until its closing). With a classic Americana '50s/'60s vibe to everything from the food and fireworks to the crafts and

ANCHOR HOCKING, A LANCASTER STALWART

https://www.anchorhocking.com/

American made for over 115 years, the Anchor Hocking company has produced glassware that's served generations of ice cream sundaes and, of course, banana splits. Still in operation in Lancaster, the company offers, among its wide product line, both the Vintage Fountainware Footed Glass Sherbet Dish and the Vintage Fountainware Glass Banana Split Dish, harkening back to the time when the ice cream icons were invented, around the same time the company was founded by Isaac Jacob Collins. Originally named for the nearby Hocking River, the Hocking Glass Company merged with the Anchor Cap and Closure Corporation in 1937, combining the operations' names. After a series of acquisitions, the company is now a subsidiary of the Oneida Group, continuing to provide "durable and design-inspired glass products for cooking, entertaining, and home decor."

car show, live music, rides and games, the family-friendly festival is also a fundraiser, with the Wilmington Rotary Club serving as the main host among other "Top Banana" sponsors. A charitable 5K even lets you run off some of the day's indulgence in preparation for the banana split eating contest.

As for the rivalry? The towns have embraced one another's claim and festivals—Latrobe's is held annually in August—serving as bookends for a summer spent enjoying the treat for which they share a mutual affection. Mayors of both cities have been known to keep up the friendly banter, inviting one another to their respective festivals and maintaining a debate as sweet in nature as its subject.

Inside Scoop: It's All About How You Slice It (The Banana Royale)

Less boat, more sundae, the banana royale was also created in 1904 (the same year as Strickler's split) by Letty Lally, who was working at Foeller's Drug Store in Columbus. When a customer requested "something different," Lally created a sundae made with banana slices, cut crosswise like coins instead of a vertical split. The ice cream chain Baskin Robbins still serves up a Banana Royale Sundae, with two scoops (one less than the split), one topping, whipped cream, nuts, a cherry and, of course, a sliced banana

GOOD HUMOR AND THE FIRST ICE CREAM TRUCK

https://www.goodhumor.com/

While the early 1900s saw a plethora of ice cream innovations—from soda fountain creations to delivery mechanisms like the cone and the popsicle— it was the 1920s that ushered in a new group of novelties and, along with them, a new way of bringing ice cream to the masses: the eternally iconic ice cream truck.

Candy shop owner Harry Burt of Youngstown, Ohio, had gotten word of another new ice cream invention, Christian Nelson's Eskimo Pie, which the fellow candy shop owner had developed after a boy in his store wanted both an ice cream and a chocolate bar but didn't have money for both. Nelson partnered with chocolate producer Russell Stover to mass produce the treats, originally named I-Scream Bars, under a new moniker given by Stover's wife, Clara, the Eskimo Pie, thus creating the Eskimo Pie Corporation. (The patent would fail to hold up, however; it was invalidated in 1928 due to its breadth and failure to describe the coating's proprietary formula.) Nelson franchised production of the product to maximize sales, which reached one million per day in 1922. Though the brand has been sold multiple times, it endured over one hundred years, until, in 2020, the current owner, Dreyer's, a division of Nestlé, announced it would be renamed the Edy's Pie to remove the potentially offensive stereotype and honor Dreyer's founder, candy maker Joseph Edy.

Harry Burt's legacy would be slightly less charged, though not without at least some drama of its own. An experienced candy maker, Burt was inspired to experiment with covering a cut block of ice cream in a smooth chocolate coating he had developed. When his daughter Ruth complained that it was too messy, his son Harry Jr. suggested they add a wooden stick, effectively turning it into a lollipop. Excited about his product, billing it as "a new, clean, convenient way to eat ice cream," Burt chose the name "Good Humor" as a nod to the popular nineteenth-century belief that a person's temperament, or "humor of the mind," was regulated by their taste, or "humor of the palate."

Enhancing the product's convenience, Burt not only sold the bars in his shop but also brought them directly to customers, adding both a refrigerator and the bell from his children's bobsled to his truck and driving around nearby neighborhoods. The idea gained popularity as quickly as the treat itself, allowing Burt to purchase twelve refrigerated trucks and set up distribution, employing drivers, known as chauffeurs, outfitted in white uniforms, who became known as Good Humor men. Required to salute gentlemen and tip their hats to ladies, Good Humor men were held to a high standard, furthered by the company's training program, which included a three-day orientation and handbook titled "Making Good at Good Humor." During peak season, drivers worked eighty-hour weeks solely on commission but were so successful, they commonly brought home over $100 per week (approximately $2,000 adjusted to today's value).

Burt filed for patents of the product, process and machinery and waited three years, eventually taking a trip to Washington, D.C., with a five-gallon pail full of Good Humor bars for officials to sample before granting their approval of the process and machinery. As the product patent was never granted, the Popsicle Corporation, founded between 1923 (the same year as Burt's patent) and 1924, battled the Good Humor Corporation in court, finally settling in a licensing agreement in 1925. Burt's widow, Cora, would reserve the licensing agreement with Popsicle upon selling the company two years after his 1926 death. While she also retained the rights to produce the Good Humor product in Youngstown and the Mahoning Valley, the family closed their main facility the following year, with Ruth's husband, Paul Bolton, taking over the candy side of the business.

The Good Humor Corporation was sold to New York businessman M.J. Meehan in 1930 and stayed in the Meehan family until 1961, when it was sold to Lipton Foods, a Unilever company. Under Lipton's ownership, the business pivoted away from direct-to-consumer sales, instead focusing on grocers and freezer cases, thus retiring the fleet of Good Humor ice cream trucks (which, at its height, had numbered over two thousand). Further acquisitions in the late '80s and early '90s paired Good Humor with the Breyers Ice Cream brand in its current iteration, the Good Humor-Breyers Company (which, around the same time, also purchased Isaly's Klondike Bar, another Ohio invention—more to come on that shortly).

We can all thank Harry Burt, the Mahoning Valley man who, well ahead of his time when it came to both product standardization and food delivery, created an icon both in product and brand and, in many ways, paved the path for today's trends in mobile culinary operations.

Inside Scoop: Promoting Good Humor for All

1929: Thomas J. Brimer, a Detroit territory Good Humor franchise owner, opened his second plant in Chicago, the Windy City, then widely controlled by the local mob. Brimer refused the mob's demand of a $5,000 payment for protection (equal to roughly $70,000 today), and the group exploded eight of his trucks. The story put Good Humor on the front page of the newspaper, increasing awareness of the brand.

1950: Jack Carson starred in the feature motion picture *The Good Humor Man*, in which "an ice-cream seller unwittingly gets involved with a femme-fatale, leading to murder-charges, gangsters and factory payroll robberies." Good Humor was no stranger to Hollywood, often parking trucks outside of motion picture studios to attract publicity and appearing in over two hundred movies.

1960: Good Humor's product lineup featured eighty-five flavors and combinations. While Burt's original Good Humor Suckers featured only chocolate-coated vanilla or chocolate, over the years, the company added strawberry as well as coatings ranging from toasted almond to coconut, chocolate cake, éclair and strawberry shortcake. Summer's biggest holiday, the Fourth of July, was celebrated with a red, white and blue Good Humor offering. Less successful specials included Oregon prune, California fig and even an experimental tomato sherbet.

Isaly's: A Skyscraper of a Swiss Story and King of the Klondike

https://isalys.com/

The picturesque hills of Monroe County reminded Swiss immigrants of their homeland, bringing many to the settlement of Switzer Township. One such family, the Isalys, immigrated in 1833, bringing with them the family's most prized possession, a copper cheese kettle.

Settling in Mansfield, Christian Isaly realized the land wasn't ideal for making cheese, so he turned to dairy farming, selling his milk to hotels and restaurants. Generations of Isalys carried on his legacy, delivering bottled milk door to door in horse-drawn carts. In 1904, the family purchased their first dairy plant, the Mansfield Pure Milk Company, and subsequently opened Isaly's Dairy Company stores in the early 1920s to sell their farm-fresh dairy products (milk, cheese, butter) as well as a variety of deli meats and an iconic treat, ice cream.

As a point of pride, the shops offered dozens of flavors, with freezer cases specially designed to hold more than their competitors. Embracing hard work, generosity and, most of all, innovation, the Isalys experimented with flavors like Chocolate Chip with the Jimmys, which replaced chocolate chips with sprinkles, as well as unique delivery mechanisms, such as slices of ice cream and holiday ice cream cakes that contained hidden designs like a Thanksgiving turkey or Christmas tree.

Perhaps Isaly's most enduring product (though the brand has been sold and no longer bears the family name), is the original Klondike Bar, invented in 1922. The innovation was the result of a group of family members' desire to simplify the ice cream bar, removing the stick. Prior to automation, original Klondike Bars were handmade and individually wrapped by Isaly's plant workers, who, being mostly female, were affectionately called "Klondike Girls." At one point, Klondikes were even used as a promotional tool, with some including a surprise pink center, which meant the customer received a free Klondike on their next visit.

Serving up a Skyscraper Valerie Lavin, 1965's Miss Ohio celebrates National Dairy Month at Isaly's Youngstown plant salesroom. *HHC Detre L&A, Gaylord LaMond Collection, 1996.329, by way of Brian Butko.*

But it was the sheer size of an Isaly's cone that brought much notoriety; in Isaly's heyday, the company became known as the "Home of the Big Cone." Originally meant to draw customers in for smaller purchases at the Mansfield plant, opened in 1910, the tall cone grew in popularity and sophistication after Isaly's bought the rights to a pointy scoop design made by the Rainbow Company in 1929. Sam Jennings, who designed and produced many serving products for Isaly's, applied for a patent on the design in 1934, assigning it to the Isaly Dairy Company. While the term *skyscraper* had been used by other companies previously, Isaly's leveraged it in advertising in 1947, and the two became synonymous. Twice the size of an average scoop (four ounces instead of two), the Skyscraper towered four full inches above the cone, giving it equal parts visual and taste appeal.

Equally as legendary as its creation was its demise: one of the owners is said to have buried all the Skyscraper scoops under the parking lot at the Boulevard Plant in Pittsburgh when Isaly's stores there were closed.

Isaly's grew quickly in the early years, opening stores throughout Ohio and neighboring West Virginia and western Pennsylvania. Signature favorites such as baked ham, bologna and still-popular Chipped Chopped Ham gained an almost equal following to Isaly's Old Fashioned Ice Cream. Fan-favorite flavors such as White House Cherry (bright white vanilla base with maraschino cherries) and Maricopa (vanilla with swirls of butterscotch) became Isaly's icons, alongside classics like vanilla, chocolate and mint chocolate chip. Two long-missed flavors, Chocolate Marshmallow and Chocolate Almond Fudge, were even brought back in 2021 and 2020, respectively, at the request of loyalists. When Isaly's ice cream was reintroduced at grocery stores in 2017, the packaging was designed to pay homage to the Isaly family heritage, featuring a Swiss boy holding a giant ice cream cone.

Scoops and Spades: The Zeroll Ice Cream Dipper

https://zeroll.com/

It may not be the Skyscraper, but another scoop with Ohio roots is equally remembered for its innovative importance. In 1932, a Toledo man named Sherman Kelly thought he was going for a scoop of ice cream while on vacation in West Palm Beach, Florida. But Sherman got more than a refreshing treat as he took note of the blisters on the hand of the young woman serving his dip; he got a business idea. Returning home, Sherman designed and patented the Zeroll Ice Cream Dipper, a "non-mechanical ice cream scoop, made of cast aluminum, with fluid inside the handle." The design used heat from the scooper's hand to warm the fluid, thereby defrosting the dipper and making the ice cream easier to scoop (it also rolled the ice cream into a ball, allowing for 10 to 20 percent more servings per gallon, a big selling point when it was introduced during the Great Depression).

Though the company sold thousands of scoops in its first year as the Zeroll Co. (1936), production was limited during World War II, forcing the company into dormancy from 1939 to 1945. Sherman's son Ralph and business partner Noel Dowling revived the business in 1946, one of the first companies to obtain aluminum after the war. The pair also expanded operations to meet the demands of the growing home market, producing scoops without fluid in the handles.

From 1953 to 1968, Ralph operated the business, changing the name to Roll Dippers during this period, before selling to Tom and Art Funka, who would eventually change its name back in 1981, then relocate the company to Fort Pierce, Florida, in 1990, bringing the product full circle to the state of its initial concept. The company, now a subsidiary of the Legacy Companies, based in Fort Lauderdale, carries on the heritage of the brand name as a "pioneer in the world of smallwares," with the Museum of Modern Art even adding the Zeroll Scoop to its Humble Masterpieces permanent collection in 2004.

At its height, Isaly's had four hundred stores and eleven plants across Ohio, Indiana and Pennsylvania. It sustained growth even during World War II, supplying provisions to the troops overseas, and sales of chopped chipped ham grew even further upon the troops' return. But due to dairy industry consolidation spanning the 1950s, '60s and '70s, plants and stores began closing. While the last Ohio store going by the name Isaly's, located in Marion, closed in 1995, the Isaly family ultimately retired in the 1980s, after selling the company to longtime provisioners and friends the Deily family.

In 2015, Tim Deily sold the brand to industry veterans Jim and Leslee Conroy of Conroy Foods Inc., who have carried on the core product offerings with a focus on the quality long associated with the Isaly's name. Passionate about the business and committed to preserving Isaly's iconic recipes. the Conroys have secured distribution in grocery chains such as Giant Eagle, as well as independent stores throughout central and northeastern Ohio.

Certainly among the first and finest in the state's ice cream industry, Isaly's became an icon for generations of Ohioans, and this new chapter allows them to carry it on for future generations. Quite the lasting legacy brought from the Swiss Alps to the hills of Ohio nearly two hundred years ago.

Inside Scoop: Scooping Up Even More History

Author Brian Butko (also the director of publications at the Heinz History Center, a Smithsonian affiliate in Pittsburgh) has quite literally written the book(s) on Isaly's: two, actually. *The Story of Isaly's: Klondikes, Chipped Ham and Skyscraper Cones*, published in 2001, and his 2021 follow-up, *Isaly's Chipped Ham, Klondikes, and Other Tales from Behind the Counter*, cover over three decades of the loyalist's dedicated research into the "world's largest dairy store chain."

His favorite way to remember the brand's proper spelling? The mnemonic "I Shall Always Love You Sweetheart = Isaly's," which was originally used in the company's advertising.

Find more from Brian and Isaly's at https://www.brianbutko.com/.

ERLENBUSCH ICE CREAM STORE AND ICE CREAM MOLDS

For ninety-eight years, the Erlenbusch Ice Cream Store (eventually named R.H. Erlenbusch & Son Co.) proudly anchored the corner of Livingston Avenue and High Street, welcoming Columbus locals as well as visitors arriving off boats from the nearby feeder canal. Born in 1937, just six years after that canal was built, Robert Erlenbusch had grown up in the thriving town, getting his first taste of the sweet life while apprenticing at P. Ambos and Company, a bakery and confectionary at High and Gay Streets.

A twenty-two-year-old Robert started his business alongside his family, marrying Dorothea Schock and making their home above the ice cream parlor, with their sons, Herman and Robert C., and daughter, Elizabeth. Robert and his sons sourced ingredients from local farmers, filling a wheelbarrow with cream and bringing in ice cut from the Scioto River and Franklin Park Lake. Making everything by hand, the Erlenbusches cooked vanilla beans daily and added seasonal fruits and berries to make strawberry, cherry, black walnut and their most famous flavor, peach, in two- to five-gallon batches. They marketed their products as "Purity" ice cream in advertising, including ads in the yearbook of old South High School, where generations of Erlenbusches were students.

The parlor itself was a gathering place, initially featuring a small fountain that looked like a little house and then, in 1870, an elaborate soda fountain imported from Green of Philadelphia, from which Erlenbusch also introduced Columbus to the ice cream soda (which Robert McCay Green is credited with inventing around the same time). Patrons visiting Erlenbusch's to celebrate a dance, recital, graduation or wedding were amazed by the fountain's flavorful array, featuring classics such as chocolate, lemon and strawberry as well as flavors somewhat lost to time: nectar, claret and sarsaparilla.

On the bakery side of the business, Robert became known for his beautifully decorated wedding cakes as well as ladyfingers, coconut macaroons and an assortment of German holiday cookies, including lebkuchen, pfeffernuss and springerle. Equally as detailed, the shop's candies, both chocolates and colorfully decorated marzipan, were made in molds.

For special occasions, the ice cream received similar treatment, hand-packed into pewter ice cream molds ranging in shapes from pineapples to ears of corn, pumpkins, turkeys and even St. Nicholas. But flowers were the most common—roses, chrysanthemums, daisies and lilies—each made with a different flavor of ice cream and arranged in a molded oval basket, often the centerpiece of a delighted child's birthday party in the 1890s.

This painstaking labor of love spoke to the dedication to quality the Erlenbusch family carried through three generations, with Robert H.'s grandchildren, Florence, Robert and Carl, taking over in the 1920s. With production reaching 1,500 gallons daily at this time, four large trucks were needed to maintain the operation's bustling delivery business.

SPEAKING OF SODA FOUNTAINS

https://wittichscandyshop.com/

One soda fountain that was originally installed at the near-opposite end of High Street from Erlenbusch's in Columbus's Beechwold neighborhood can be found today in Circleville at the state's and the nation's oldest family-owned and -operated candy shop.

Wittich's, established in 1840 (that's 182 years ago, if you're counting), became the soda fountain's new home in 1997, after the closure of the Beechwold Pharmacy, the last pharmacy to have an operational soda fountain in Columbus. Fred Wittich, great-grandson of Gottlieb F. Wittich, the confectionary's founder, purchased the soda fountain after being introduced to the pharmacy's owner, Arden Englebach, by Bob Eagle of Eagle Family Candy, whose shop is located just a block from the old pharmacy.

Behind the scenes at Beechwold Pharmacy. *Arden and Pat Engelbach, by way of Shirley Hyatt.*

Above: Full view of the original soda fountain counter. *Arden and Pat Engelbach, by way of Shirley Hyatt.*

Left: Pat Engelbach pulls the last soda at Beechwold Pharmacy. *Arden and Pat Engelbach, by way of Shirley Hyatt.*

It took Fred and his wife, Janet, three days to disassemble the fountain, bring it down to their shop and have a plumber install each component. Arden and his wife, Pat, also came down, helping train Wittich's employees on how to make sodas the old-fashioned way and even bringing a recipe book that came with the soda fountain.

Frank, who came to consider himself less an owner of the business and more "a curator of a piece of history," passed away in 2015, but his wife and three children carry on Wittich's tradition of candy-making excellence and steward the shop's soda fountain, which now touts a topper of "Wittichs Beechwold Fountain."

In March 1957, Erlenbusch's served its last ice cream soda as the fourth generation pursued other career opportunities, and Florence and Carl chose to retire. Preserving the family's legacy, the shop's classic walnut tables and cane-seat chairs, as well as memorabilia, were sold to loyal customers, with ice cream-making equipment, such as the molds, donated to the Ohio Historical Society (they sit today in the Museum Collection at the Ohio History Connection). From serving that first ice cream soda eighty-seven years prior, the fountain found its way to New York City, carrying on its own legacy somewhere in Queens.

ASHLAND SANITARY DAIRY

Situated almost directly between Columbus and Cleveland, Ashland is a small yet bustling town with the motto "The World Headquarters of Nice People." Perhaps it should also be "ice" people, as it's long been home to dairies, the most popular of which dates back to 1913. The Ashland Sanitary Dairy, started by W.D. Cummings and Stewart Whitcomb, was well placed at 161 Center Street, quickly building a client base in the central business location.

In 1917, Cliff Gongwer and David M. Reed bought into the business, taking it over completely just two years later. In 1925, the pair purchased from the parents of Cliff's wife, Florence, a farm (sixty-five acres within the city limits) of purebred Guernsey cows, who produced the dairy's signature Grade A milk. A reputation for healthier processing and customer service led the company to welcome visitors into the dairy to view the plant and its processes.

From milk to butter, whipping cream to cottage cheese, the dairy produced a variety of products both onsite and via direct delivery to customers' homes. Its "Delicious Ice Milk Frozen Dessert"—available in half gallons of vanilla, chocolate or strawberry; in the form of ice cream novelties; and in special-occasion molds, center bricks and stenciled bricks—offered treats for every day as well as celebrations.

In 1934, a retail store was added and became a popular hangout for local teens throughout the '40s and '50s. With retail and wholesale combined, the operation extended as far as one hundred miles outside of Ashland (shipping via the Southwestern railroad), and total annual production was 300,000 pounds of butter and 75,000 gallons of ice cream, while daily milk sales reached 1,500 gallons. During this heyday, the operation leveraged a fleet of nine trucks and employed thirty people.

Cliff bought out David in 1948 and brought in his brother-in-law, Jack Lentz Sr., who worked at the store making toppings such as hot fudge and butterscotch, roasting nuts and freezing popsicles. In addition to ice cream, the dairy featured a menu of favorites such as grilled cheese and cream of tomato soup.

In the mid-1960s, a merger between Ashland Sanitary Dairy and the Boyer Dairy created the new All-Star Dairy, relocated to 725 Clark Street. Around the same time, the original Center Street location suffered damage due to a fire but was used as the headquarters for Ashland's sesquicentennial celebration. Two years later, in 1967, a Hawkin's market was opened on the site by Earl Hawkins. While that location is now a Save a Lot, Hawkins went on to open a Claremont Avenue location in 1974, which, after a few ownership changes in the late 1990s and early 2000s, lives on as part of Miller's Markets (started in Wauseon, Ohio) since 2017.

From its days of dairy wagons to iterations of local locations, the Ashland Sanitary Dairy stayed rooted in its promise of doing things "the modern and sanitary way," something we might now take for granted when it comes to our milk production but that was, at the time, well ahead of its time.

Sweet Moses Soda Fountain & Treat Shop

Not quite as old as its counterparts described thus far in this book and with a run that ended much more recently, Sweet Moses Soda Fountain & Treat Shop touts not one but two "firsts": being named for the founding father of Cleveland, Moses Cleaveland, and being the first shop in the state to serve vegan ice cream, something that was relatively new when the shop opened in March 2011. But whether dairy-free or not, fans of the shop are sure to miss more than the ice cream, as the shop has shuttered after a strong decade-long run, ending the old-fashioned soda fountain experience that many came to have for the first time and others to remember from long ago.

Jeff Moreau, formerly an advertising professional with a background in creating customer experiences, was seeking a new path when he realized a passion for the food and beverage industry that he'd cultivated during stints working in restaurants in both high school and college. Wanting to focus on a concept without a liquor license or hot stations such as a fryer or grill top, he tapped into his lifelong love of chillier foods, specifically ice cream, thinking it might be simpler. But when Jeff stumbled upon and fell deep into the history of soda fountains, hitting upon the idea of creating a

Serving up a sweet taste of the past in modern-day Cleveland. *Sweet Moses Ltd.*

unique experience specialized for the market, he went full bore, sourcing antiques to establish the atmosphere and recreating recipes from his mom's old cookbooks for everything on the menu—from ice cream and toppings to baked goods, chocolates, caramel corn and even root beer.

Inspired by the proof of concept in the success of Franklin Fountain in Philadelphia, Jeff started with the idea to create a neighborhood soda fountain in greater Cleveland. At the time, a revitalization project was just beginning in the Gordon Square Arts District, which housed an old storefront location perfectly suited to his needs. "I didn't open because I thought there wasn't good ice cream in Cleveland; there's quite a bit, actually," says Jeff, adding, "I wanted more of an ice cream dessert experience, something more special than sitting outside with the little league team and good for the locals but also a bit of a destination."

And that it certainly became, with customers often traveling from suburbs forty-five minutes outside of the city for special occasion trips and people who hadn't been to the neighborhood in many years stopping by (the shop was also a stop on the Ohio Ice Cream Trail after it was created in 2015). Because of the shop's multigenerational appeal, grandparents were able to share the taste and experience—many commenting on how they hadn't had a chocolate soda since they were a teenager—with their grandchildren, who were incredulous at the idea they had ever been that young. "Those moments were really special," recalls Jeff. "Ice cream is something a grandma and a five-year-old can always agree on."

And who wouldn't agree with Sweet Moses's approach to being as authentic an old-fashioned fountain as possible? From sauces, like caramel and hot fudge, to whipped cream, everything was fresh and true to its original form. In a nod to the lost art of the soda jerk, the shop even hand-carbonated all of its sodas, from plain Cokes to those used for ice cream sodas and phosphates. Enhancing the blast from the past, Jeff consulted the *Dispenser's Formulary*, a soda fountain handbook published in 1905, to present long-lost favorites from the New York Egg Cream and Canadian Frost Bite to the Razzle Dazzle and Strawberry Paulette.

Rather than extend themselves too far in terms of flavor offerings, Jeff preferred to focus on a core of about fourteen flavors, which served as the base for creativity in his lineup of signature sundaes. In addition to the ever-popular Tin Roofs and Turtles, Jeff's personal favorite was the Ballpark Sundae, a Cracker Jack–inspired matchup of Salted French Caramel ice cream on a bed of crunchy, homemade caramel corn, topped with homemade hot fudge, more caramel corn, Spanish peanuts, whipped cream and a cherry. The new instant classic, which Jeff described as "a combination of sweet and salty, crunchy and creamy," was enjoyed by many Cleveland fans when Sweet Moses had an outpost at Progressive Field, home of the Indians (now Guardians) baseball team, from 2015 through 2021.

In addition to the classic vanilla bean and chocolate (both also available in vegan versions), featured flavors included favorites like cookies and cream, mint chocolate chip and strawberry. On the more inventive side, Coconut Almond Chocolate Chip and Bananas Foster were both menu mainstays, with the latter including twenty bananas in each batch, a homemade cinnamon caramel sauce swirled throughout and a hint of Myers's dark rum.

Regarding the vegan offering, Jeff says, "I first did it for lactose-intolerant people, not even really realizing the growing vegan customer base. Interest grew over the life of the business, and people loved that they could make a whole vegan sundae adding toppings to suit their preferences."

With the goal of inviting customers to step back in time, all of Sweet Moses's furnishings and equipment were for actual use, not just for looks. From the authentic 1940s Bastion-Blessings soda fountain, framed in sixteen feet of Tennessee marble, to the wrought-iron ice cream chairs and, of course, the vintage glassware used to serve up sundaes and sodas, plus wall art of vintage Cleveland postcards, stepping in truly felt like stepping back. Even the house-made hot chocolate was made using a recipe from 1911.

"It was very much a passion project," says Jeff, adding, "I did everything I wanted to; some of it didn't make sense, but I did it anyway." And while he did seek a buyer to carry on the brand in the building that he owned, in the end, it was time to close up shop when he and his wife decided to relocate after her 2021 retirement. "I believe we had an impact on the neighborhood while we were here, and we're leaving it a better place," says Jeff, and customers emphatically agree, with his announcement post on social media reaching over 250,000 people and garnering nearly nine hundred comments. The show of support at the shop was every bit as evident when closing weekend came around, bringing lines of customers who waited two and a half hours to purchase everything but the fixtures—chocolates, toppings and even entire two-and-a-half-gallon tubs of ice cream.

Similar to its namesake, who only spent a short time in the city after founding it, Sweet Moses had a short, memorable presence in the city, becoming entwined with the fabric of the area quickly due to the older and more established feeling of the overall experience. Jeff wishfully foresees a future where locals will say to one another, "Do you remember Sweet Moses?" and fond memories of celebrations, including engagements, engagement photo shoots and wedding parties, will be shared again, even if only as stories.

As for Jeff's next stop? Small business owners stand to benefit from his learning, as he hopes to be involved with mentoring, teaching and sharing with other entrepreneurs, including minority business owners looking to get their start and bring their dreams to life.

Sweet Moses was a truly special place for special occasions and brought a special sense of nostalgia, continuing Ohio's long legacy of passionate ice cream proprietors, among whom Jeff certainly deserves a special place.

Inside Scoop: A Simpler Spelling

Notice something slightly off about Mr. Moses's surname on page 31? It's not a typo but rather the correct spelling of the city founder's last name. It is said to have been shortened when the *Cleveland Advertiser*, a local paper in the early 1800s, couldn't fit the full version on its masthead, so it dropped the extra *a* to make room. Rumor has it the early American wasn't entirely happy with the decision, which is why he's infamously scowling in virtually every portrait and statue made of him. Sweet Moses's website used to jest that his frown might have turned upside down if he'd had a chance to try the shop's ice cream.

Chapter 2

A FAMILY AFFAIR

While generational businesses were common when ice cream got its start, the carrying on of a legacy through lineage has grown to be a formidable challenge in more recent times. Historically, about 40 percent of family-owned businesses in the United States have been passed down to the second generation, typically the owners' children, while only 13 percent transition successfully to a third generation. When it comes to the fourth generation? A mere 3 percent transition successfully, which makes those that do last this long stand out, both for their tenacity (as these companies weather many societal and financial ups and downs) and commitment to the quality of their offering.

In Ohio, families have grown the ice cream industry as much as the ice cream industry has grown families. Across the state, the early Aglamesises and Graeters set up shop in the neighborhoods of Cincinnati, while the Dietsch brothers, the Handels and the Pierres chose Cleveland and northeastern Ohio to build their legacies. Generations of central Ohioans have enjoyed cups and cones at Velvet's Ye Olde Mill, Young's Jersey Dairy and Tom's Ice Cream Bowl, while the suburbs of Columbus welcomed Johnson's and Whit's.

Family is not only what started these companies and what has carried them through the decades (in some cases, even a century), but it's also what fuels their continued focus. Ultimately, the business of making ice cream is the business of one family facilitating the happiness of another, that of the customer, who, in turn, returns time and time again for their favorite flavor and a shared experience of good old-fashioned fun.

AGLAMESIS BROTHERS

https://www.aglamesis.com/

Walking into Aglamesis Bro.'s storefront in the Oakley neighborhood of Cincinnati is equal parts a time warp to the early 1900s and a trip to the place that inspired the shop's design, New Orleans. Third-generation owner Randall "Randy" Young carries on the 114-year-old legacy with origins even farther away—in Sparta, Greece.

It was from there that Thomas Aglamesis, just sixteen years old, left home after the passing of his father made him the head of the family and thus financially responsible. Seeking opportunity in America, Thomas settled in Cincinnati, and within a year, his brother Nicholas joined him. The two worked within the "Old Arcade" downtown, learning the ice cream trade and saving up to open their own shop. Originally named the Metropolitan, their first ice cream parlor opened in 1908 in the community of Norwood. Using rock salt and metal cylinders, they churned all of their own ice cream by hand in the basement of the building (it wasn't until 1921 that they purchased a machine for the task). They also delivered to neighboring homes, developing a reputation for having "the fastest horse team in town." To expand their offering and offset the seasonality of their product, the brothers added confections shortly thereafter.

Just five years later, in 1913, they expanded their footprint, adding a second location in the Oakley community, a classic, beautiful space made of imported Portuguese marble, tile floors, sculptured ceilings and Tiffany lamps. The space, with its an authentic player piano, brought east-siders in for both its ambiance and offerings, quickly becoming a gathering place, as it remains today.

During the Great Depression, the brothers sold their original shop, along with the Metropolitan name, to colleagues, leaving the Oakley parlor as their primary location and namesake. The business weathered both the economic downtown as well as World War II, even through sugar rations that affected production capacity and slowed growth.

In the 1950s, after the death of Nicholas and health struggles of Thomas, the business passed to James "Jim" Aglamesis, Thomas's son. Maintaining the Old World techniques and recipes to keep a consistent product, Jim was inspired by his 1965 honeymoon to New Orleans to renovate the shop, borrowing from New Orleans's wrought-iron balconies and bringing in the pink color scheme. He opened a second location in 1970 in the Montgomery neighborhood, keeping the same look and feel for its interior.

Aglamesis parlor, circa the 1920s. *Aglamesis Brothers.*

While the ice cream itself stayed the same, Jim—"Mr. A.," as he became known in later years—also gleaned menu inspiration from his trip, adding sundaes such as the Basin Street (French Vanilla and Dutch Holland Chocolate wallowing in marshmallow and hot fudge) and the iconic Bourbon Street (French Vanilla, Dutch Holland Chocolate and coffee ice creams covered in bittersweet, marshmallow and caramel). Within the special menu section, there's also a nod—dubbed "For the Monkey In You"—to the Orleans Royal: French Vanilla and Dutch Holland Chocolate covered in hot fudge, chocolate whipped cream, walnuts—and did we mention the banana? But for the purists, not to worry: the Banana Classique is "a more traditional banana split," with vanilla, chocolate and strawberry ice creams; chocolate, strawberry and pineapple sauces; whipped cream (which is scooped instead of sprayed from a can in another nod to the old-fashioned style); and crushed walnuts. Bringing a bigger appetite—or a crowd? Consider the French Quarter "Petite," featuring four large scoops of a variety of ice cream flavors (customers' choice, if preferred) "swimming in Marshmallow, Caramel, and Hot Fudge Sauces, with a banana, pyramids of whipped cream and generously garnished with nuts." Still not quite enough? Go all out for the French Quarter Bonanza, a similar setup upgraded to eight scoops!

The ice cream parlor classics are there, too: milkshakes and malts, egg creams, phosphates and sodas (including another nod to NOLA, the "Nectar Soda," a New Orleans–style cream soda). But in an Aglamesis twist, sodas are served up either "Sincere" (one scoop) or "Extra Sincere" (two scoops). The term isn't just a fun naming mechanism but rather a brand and family value, according to Randy, who took over from his stepfather, Jim, after his nearly seventy years of leadership, to carry on the allegiance to quality. "We maintain an emphasis on the experience as well as the product," says Randy. "We use bananas [for longtime favorite Banana Ice Cream]; we use strawberries [for his personal favorite, the Strawberry Chocolate Chip]. We use the same chocolate in our ice cream that we use to make our candy. And most importantly, we want people to come in and visit, spend time with their families and create memories."

And generations of memories have certainly been created at Aglamesis, from prom dates to engagements. In fact, Mr. A. was such a part of the community, until his passing in 2021 at the age of ninety-three, that the city council voted later that year to designate Allston Street as James T. Aglamesis Way. And it's this community that Randy credits with Aglamesis having been continuously in business in the same parlor for over a century. "Ohioans are friendly people that like to gather," he says. And what's more, "The big secret of Ohio is that the three Cs [Cincinnati, Columbus, Cleveland] have great culinary backgrounds rich with immigration. At the turn of the nineteenth century, there were Greeks, Italians, Germans coming, and if they weren't sponsored by someone, they went into grocery and restaurant businesses."

Randy continues the family's legacy alongside sister Dianne Lytle and now the fourth generation, his daughter Kristi Weissman. The trio maintains a dual focus on quality, expanding confectionery production in 2022 to an offsite location, and the experience, considering an expansion to more locations in the Cincinnati area (customers have only been asking for the last fifty-plus years!). But Randy emphasizes that even if some things change, the important things will stay the same: making ice cream and candy the "sincere" way, as they have since the very beginning.

Inside Scoop: The Other Side of the Counter at Aglamesis

Even if you came in for the ice cream, the candy case will call you before you leave Aglamesis. Pack up a box of these classics for when your sugar high wears off.

- Hand-dipped Cordial Cherries
- Classic East Coast Opera Creams, featuring a unique style of fondant enrobing a vanilla center
- Sea Salt Caramels
- Giant Pecandes
- Mocha Cream (the newest addition, after an employee suggested blending coffee with chocolate; it spent two years in research and development before it was perfected)

GRAETER'S

https://www.graeters.com/

Over 150 years ago, Richard Graeter's great-grandfather Louis Charles Graeter began selling ice cream from carts at Cincinnati's street markets. It was 1870, and ice cream was a novelty, as well as a very manual process, with hardworking young Louis handcrafting it in French pots, the standard at the time.

After a brief detour to Washington state, during which he left the business in the hands of his brother Fred, Louis returned to Cincinnati in 1900, reclaiming the business and meeting Regina Berger, who would become his third wife and, ultimately, the "Boss" of both the family and the business. The couple moved to the new upscale neighborhood of Walnut Hills, where they made ice cream in the back of their home and sold it in the front parlor; they and their two sons lived upstairs.

But in 1919, tragedy struck the family when Louis was killed by an automobile, leaving Regina and now-teenage Wilmer and Paul to determine the fate of their father's nearly fifty-year-old business. Strong-willed even in a time when women rarely ran companies and in the face of both the end of World War I and the Spanish flu pandemic, Regina remained tough, making the savvy decision to open Graeter's storefronts throughout the city's neighborhoods (starting with Hyde Park in 1922), while retaining centralized production. This cost-saving technique allowed for rapid expansion, but Regina's most critical decision came a few years later, with the 1926 invention of the continuous freezer. This device was cheaper and quicker than a French pot, so many ice cream makers opted to modernize over time, but Regina felt the result was too light, preferring the density and melt of the original method (18 percent butterfat also lends to the indulgent creaminess).

Far from the family parlor of the early 1900s, Graeter's today boasts locations throughout the state, like this beautiful brick building near Columbus. *Graeter's.*

So, Graeter's soldiered on, two-and-a-half gallons at a time, just as it does today. Alongside their mother, both sons contributed greatly to the expansion of the operation, with Paul adding bakeries into the ice cream parlors to offset winter sales slumps and Wilmer creating Graeter's signature process for making larger-than-typical chocolate chips. As the family legend goes, Graeter's had also always been a candy company, at least since 1900, and Regina made all the candy, dipping it by hand and swirling the tops. Sometime in the '40s or '50s, Wilmer was running the ice cream room and thought to take a quart of his mother's chocolate, add a little bit of vegetable oil so it didn't get too hard and mix it into the pot. Eventually, he perfected the method, which is still used today; like the French pot method, it's more labor intensive than simply squirting in a premade chocolate sauce, but it gives Graeter's chip flavors a distinctive taste experience, due to the wide variety of sizes of these signature "chunks."

This "stubborn commitment to making the best ice cream possible," as the Graeter family fully embraces it, continued after Regina's own passing in 1955 and Paul's retirement, with Wilmer's children, Dick, Lou, Jon and Kathy. The third generation of Graeters knew the French pot machines needed updating but, of course, also needed to retain the same standard

40

of output. While the machines were refined to make them more consistent, durable and compliant with current safety standards, the batch size and process were maintained—ensuring that the flavor and texture would be, as well.

Speaking of flavor, by now, Graeter's Black Raspberry Chocolate Chip has become a fast fan favorite and is still the company's signature best seller, featuring fruit from family farms in Oregon's Willamette Valley (which also lends both fruit and its name to the brand's Oregon Strawberry). Bringing in the bakery side of the business, the signature 1870 Tower Sundae tops a fresh chocolate bundt cake filled with hot fudge with a scoop of Black Raspberry Chocolate Chip ice cream, drizzled with more hot fudge and topped with fresh whipped cream, pecans and a cherry. Beyond scoops and sundaes, other fountain menu favorites are milkshakes, malts, sodas (double or even triple dip!), smoothies and coffee chillers, featuring Graeter's ice cream blended with espresso syrup.

But it's another best seller that tops the list of now-president and CEO Richard: the Madagascar Vanilla Bean, because of its "classic, delicious and timeless flavor." Perhaps he has a soft spot for the classics due to his memories of working in the factory as a teenager in the late '70s, learning to make mixes and flavors such as seasonal staple peach, brought back

Graeter's third generation (*left to right*): Kathy, Dick and Lou. *Graeter's.*

each summer. "We peeled them by hand back then, after boiling in hot water (to release the skins)," Richard recalls, adding, "Dad, Grandpa, our maintenance guy and I sat around a table peeling peaches that were then stirred up with sugar and added to the ice cream." Though the peaches are now processed and pasteurized at the grower for uniform consistency, Richard remembers when "June peaches tasted different than July peaches." Using his grandfather's recipe book, Richard started his summer job early each day, cooking eggs, making egg custard, pouring in fruit puree. "The first flavor we made every morning was caramel," he recalls, "marrying brown sugar and cream in a copper bowl over an open flame." The machinery was a bit different then, too. Richard remembers using an old-fashioned wood paddle made of maple, which won't splinter; today's machines have a scraper. "We made every flavor every day or every other day, as the freezer wasn't very big back then, which meant the ice cream you got in the store was made the night before." Capping off his memories, Richard acknowledges, "It is an insane way to make ice cream, so labor intensive. No one else would be crazy enough, but that's all we've ever known."

As Richard and brothers Chip (chief of retail operations) and Bob (chief of quality assurance) took over from the generation before them, the company was well poised for continued growth, based both on an expanded factory, direct-to-consumer shipping (one of the first ice cream brands to leverage dry ice to do so) and a relationship with Cincinnati-based grocer Kroger, which would ultimately give Graeter's retail presence at stores across the country. And grow they have, now producing roughly 1.5 million gallons of ice cream per year, ten times as much as when Richard first worked in the business as a kid. As each machine still only makes 2.5 gallons at a time, even with forty machines, they're now running two ten-hour shifts per day to meet production demands. "We've learned how to scale up a very small, craft, batch process, keeping the artisanal quality of the product," says Richard. And in addition to multiple generations of the family working in the business, he credits having an "incredible team of non–family members to augment the family. The last name may not be Graeter, but they really are part of the family and responsible for the success of the brand."

With the number of pre-twentieth-century Cincinnati companies that are still in operation today numbering only in the dozens, according to the Ohio Manufacturers' Association, the bond between the Graeter's brand and the city that birthed it is strong. From Regina's initial expansion, the

Graeter's fourth generation (*left to right*): Chip, Richard and Bob. *Graeter's.*

number of stores grew locally to around twenty, with over fifty total across neighboring states, including Kentucky, Pennsylvania, Indiana and Illinois. "Cincinnati, and Ohio in general, are a natural fit for ice cream makers due to the abundance of dairy farms in the Midwest," says Richard, adding, "Cincinnati sits on the Ohio River and is a bustling hub for food and drink connoisseurs, as well as football and baseball fanatics. Cincinnati is home to the oldest MLB team, world-renowned chili and craft ice cream."

When it comes to the latter, the Graeter's name is certainly synonymous with Cincinnati, as much now as it has been for the past 150 years. And as the fifth generation—including Richard's daughter and son, currently in college—aspire to follow in the footsteps of their family legacy, the shoes to fill are firmly rooted in doing things the old-fashioned way, just as the "Boss" would've wanted. While the company's vision may include optimizing, its continued success lies in making ice cream the same way it has across the generations, just two-and-a-half gallons at a time. "Any successful business needs to have a point of difference, and the French pot process is really unique," says Richard. "Future generations will keep the same eye on quality, heritage and commitment as their predecessors. It is the only way we know, and it is, for those who know the difference, what makes Graeter's, well, Graeter's."

Inside Scoop: Five Fun Facts for Five Generations of Graeter's

1. Graeter's employees have the job title "ice cream artisan."
2. In 2002, Oprah Winfrey declared Graeter's the best ice cream she'd ever tasted, serving its signature vanilla to her studio audience of three hundred and skyrocketing online sales.
3. Food Network's *Top 5 Restaurants* named Graeter's Black Raspberry Chocolate Chip among the top five ice cream flavors in America.
4. The 2020 pandemic cancelled many of Graeter's 150th anniversary celebration plans, including the world's largest ice cream social, but the end of the year did bring the introduction of the Perfect Indulgence line, a vegan version of six of Graeter's traditional flavors: Black Cherry Chocolate Chip, Cookies and Cream, Oregon Strawberry, Mint Chocolate Chip, Chocolate and Chocolate Chip.
5. Graeter's is home to the world's only French pot freezer and is the last small-batch ice cream maker still dedicated to this time-honored process.

HANDEL'S

https://handelsicecream.com/

Summer 1945: gathering fruit from her backyard to use in her own personal recipes, Alice Handel developed a treat to cool the heat for her Youngstown neighbors. Word spread quickly, and Alice relocated her new operation to her husband's gas station, but even that became too busy, prompting her to move across the street, opening the first Handel's Ice Cream location, still in operation today.

Alice's sweet legacy began with a commitment to fresh, quality ingredients that is carried on today at outposts throughout Ohio, as well as nine other states. Upholding Alice's traditions, each store makes its ice cream daily, using her original methods and recipes. Loyal customers recognize this freshness and are addicted to the creamy texture and legendary taste, amplified by a generous commitment to flavor mix-ins. Jim Brown, Handel's chief operating officer, says, "You can taste and see the quality and generous portions, whether it's tossing the huge pecans into the ice cream by hand, or breaking the Oreos into large chunks."

Serving smiles since the summer of 1945. *Handel's Ice Cream.*

Those pecans are part of the Youngstown legacy, too, as many fans are loyal to the signature flavor, Chocolate Pecan, chocolate ice cream mixed with a hearty portion of roasted, buttered and salted pecans. Loyalty to one's favorite flavor can go to extremes, even those of the weather-related variety. As Jim recalls, there was a news story during a particularly cold midwestern winter in which "the wind chill was about -30 degrees with a few feet of snow on the ground, and there were still customers coming up to the window. The TV station was so intrigued by these customers that they showed up to hear their story. One gentleman said it well: 'You see, I've learned that when my wife wants Handel's Chocolate Pecan ice cream, it's in my best interest to go buy some.'"

A more widespread favorite, Graham Central Station, is popular at Handel's locations across the country; it features graham-flavored ice cream with a graham cracker ripple and chocolate-covered crunchies. And while Jim hesitates to play favorites, he acknowledges his hometown connection, saying, "Being from Ohio, our Buckeye flavor is high on my list, but some stores are not as excited about serving that flavor, where Ohio State is a football rival." Struggling to pick just one from the roughly forty-eight flavors available daily? Relief is available in the form of the 4 Scoop Sampler, a menu staple, alongside sundaes, shakes, sandwiches (of the ice cream variation, of course), Handel Pops (vanilla, chocolate or mint chocolate chip ice cream covered in rich, gourmet chocolate and served on a stick) and Hurricanes (Handel's world-famous vanilla ice cream blended with a wide array of fruit and/or candy offerings).

Handel's legacy switched hands but maintained its heart when, in the mid-1980s, Alice passed the baton to new owner Lenny Fisher. But in nearly forty years, she hadn't had time to write down her original recipes, leaving Lenny to join her early at the shop to watch her making each batch from memory and feel. Frantically, Lenny observed, measured and took notes as Alice coolly tossed in a little of this and a lot of that, figuring out each recipe to carry them forward, just as she'd perfected them over all her years. Likewise, Lenny got a crash course in machinery, as a repairman wasn't easy to find for the specific machines Alice had been using. He quickly learned the inner workings of each, becoming an expert at making the magic that makes Handel's.

Strong partnerships have been a foundation for Handel's, which has long-standing relationships with both local farms and big producers, such as Hershey's. While Reese's peanut butter cups and Hershey's syrup star in Hurricanes and hot fudge sundaes, an abundance of fresh fruit, from summer's strawberries and peaches to apples come fall, are the base of Handel's fruit flavors, developed in Alice's backyard and still some of the most popular.

Made fresh daily at each Handel's location. *Han l's Ice Cream.*

Whether they're longtime fans who've enjoyed Handel's in Ohio for decades or new faces in new markets, Handel's is committed to its customers and proud to be a part of their lives, serving as a center of each community, just as Alice did from her first location on what is now known as Hai el's Court. From devoted husbands braving the elements to get to their v es' favorite frozen flavor, to brides and grooms popping by on their wedding day to celebrate the role Handel's had in their courtship, Handel's is humbled to share those special moments.

"We've seen a lot of fads come and go through the years, and v e've learned what our customers appreciate from Handel's is classic flavors with time-tested recipes," says Jim. "We'll explore and innovate with new vors and with ways to continue improving our customer experience, but we're not changing the core of the business: ice cream with a legendary taste that's made fresh daily on site." From the sounds of it, that approach surely ould be Alice-approved.

DIETSCH BROTHERS

https://dietschs.com/

When you hear about a family-run business, you might assun e the organization has been passed down through one branch of a family's tree, but for the Dietsch family of Findlay, the roots run much wider. F two generations, multiple siblings were involved with the company's develc ment and growth, and today, a father-daughter team carries that legacy into the company's eighth decade, with her sons poised to someday continue that success into the fourth generation.

The origins of Dietsch Brothers began in 1927, when the second oldest of twelve siblings, Edward, purchased the C.W. Wickham Candy Co. With help from two of his younger brothers, Chris and Don, Edward used family recipes to expand the operation to make ice cream. Unfortunately, when Edward suffered a nose infection in 1934, penicillin had yet to be introduced in the United States, and he passed away, leaving his widow, Doris, to run the company until her own early death a few years later.

But as they came of age, Chris and Don were able to lean on the things they'd learned before Edward's passing, methods for both candy and ice cream production, and when the opportunity came to purchase the local Rogge Bakery Shop, they opened the company known today as Dietsch Brothers on December 7, 1937. Their youngest brother, Roy, would join them upon his high school graduation in 1938, completing the trio once again.

All three brothers served in the military during World War II, leaving the business in the hands of siblings and extended family. It took a true team effort to make it through tough times, including a period of sugar rationing, but the store stayed open, and when they returned home safely, the brothers worked long hours, staying open until midnight if necessary to produce enough chocolates and ice cream. Their wives joined in during

Just a few packaging changes since 1937 at Dietsch Brothers. *Dietsch Brothers.*

Dietsch Brothers gallons of flavor. *Dietsch Brothers.*

busy holiday times, and their children helped out from a young age during summer and holiday breaks. Among those children were Roy's own trio of sons, Rick, Jeff and Tom, who became involved with the organization professionally in the 1970s, after their uncle Chris's passing. Both Don and Roy would retire in the 1980s, officially passing the generational torch in 1987, though they continued to help out, as family does. In 1998, Jeff's daughter, Erika, an only child, joined the business full time and worked alongside her uncles until their respective retirements in 2012 (Rick) and 2019 (Tom). Now serving as the company's vice president, supporting Jeff as president, Erika has two sons, Evan and Logan, one or both of whom may someday help carry on the company's longstanding legacy.

That legacy is due in large part to a focus on quality over quantity, which has long been a family motto and secret to success. With just two stores, one near the heart of town and the other on the east side, Dietsch Brothers has focused on Findlay—for good reason, according to Erika. "I feel strongly that we have a great thing going on right here. Family is absolutely the most important thing and I want everyone to be able to take time off when needed and enjoy time away from work." At the heart of Hancock County in northwest Ohio, Findlay's is a big small town, and its population of over forty thousand has grown continuously over the last seven years. Ranked the top "micropolitan" community in the United States, the area boasts great schools, parks and a thriving downtown of restaurants and shops.

The original downtown location has been the same since 1956, when the brothers were able to purchase land next door to the first property they had been renting and built their own store, which has now been expanded four times. The second location, opened in 1974, doubled in size after a 2003 renovation that added a dedicated area for chocolates and gifts, enlarging the original side to feature ice cream only. Both offer an old-fashioned fountain menu that includes over thirty flavors of ice cream and five sherbets produced year-round, as well as roughly thirty seasonal flavors that rotate.

Fan favorites are noted directly in the store with a small ice cream decal on the flavor board indicating a flavor's place in the store's top ten. Vanilla leads the list, not only because it's a classic but also for its role as a base of many milkshakes and signature sundaes. It even stars in the most popular, Chocolate Milkshake, also one of Erika's favorites; as she says, "Our vanilla ice cream paired with our chocolate sauce that we make in our kitchen is the best blend of sweetness." Others high on the list include strawberry, chocolate, cookie dough, butter pecan, mint chocolate chip, Moose Tracks and, last but never least, at least not in the Buckeye State, is Dietsch's Buckeye ice cream, with that same chocolate sauce rippled throughout peanut butter ice cream and small buckeye pieces hand scattered throughout.

Sodas, phosphates and Boston coolers (a milkshake made with ginger ale in place of milk) nod to the tried-and-true nature of the business, as does a lineup of house-made signature sundae toppings, including a chocolate sauce, strawberry topping, butterscotch, marshmallow crème, maple and a bittersweet sauce. Whether you choose a classic hot fudge or go for the nostalgic taste of a Mallo-Bitter (bittersweet and marshmallow sauces), Dietsch's sundaes can all be customized with your preferred ice cream flavor and choice of "extras," ranging from nuts (peanuts, cashews, almonds or pecans), banana slices, whipped cream and, of course, sprinkles. Extra hungry? Try a classic banana split or a more modern Slim Jim, which has one less scoop of ice cream but still has all the fruit sauces (strawberry, cherry, pineapple) and adds marshmallow to the mix for a slightly "lighter" take.

Erika's go-to has always been mint chocolate chip, but she also has a soft spot for the seasonal cinnamon, her perfect pairing for her aunt Jill's skillet apple pie. Pumpkin is another fall favorite, while coconut is a sure sign of spring, welcoming snowbirds back to Ohio from their warm-weather escapes. Summer belongs to sherbet, with watermelon reigning as the most refreshing, and eggnog is a holiday staple. No matter the flavor, it all starts with an ice cream mix made specifically by Grove Dairy to have a 12 percent butterfat content, which Erika says "gives our ice cream a creamy texture without being too heavy or rich." Using two ten-gallon batch freezers and a rippler, which takes a topping like caramel or fudge and blends it into the ice cream, ice cream is produced in small batches to ensure a quick turnaround. Many flavors have what is referred to industrywide as "inclusions," ingredients such as nuts (roasted in-house), fruits such as berries, peanut butter cups, buckeye pieces and cookie dough bits, all of which are added either at the very end of the fifteen-minute cycle or by hand after it is complete to ensure even distribution and avoid mushy inclusions.

The high quality of toppings and inclusions is a direct result of the fine chocolate side of the business, which is also produced on-site. Bestseller milk chocolate–covered pretzels show up in the Chocolate Pretzel Caramel Swirl, while buckeyes take center stage in their namesake flavor. Cream centers, caramels, nut clusters, toffee squares, truffles and pecan critters (Dietsch's variation on a turtle with pecans and caramels) round out the lineup, also offering some balance to the somewhat seasonal nature of the business: holiday gifting of chocolates picks up just as summer ice cream sales start to taper off. Photos of the candy and ice cream–making process are featured at both locations to give customers a glimpse behind the scenes.

Erika credits not only her relatives, both working in and retired from the business, but also a team of managers, full- and part-time employees who are critical to and invested in Dietsch Brothers' continued success. "Some have been here for over 40 years," she says. "We hire high school students to work part time, many who come back to help during holiday and summer breaks from college. Most of our management team started working here in high school and decided to stay on full time and make this their career." She's also grateful for support throughout the years from the community and from surrounding businesses, including many major retail, manufacturing, agriculture and automotive companies that have production, distribution and even headquarters in Findlay, saying that they not only come to Dietsch Brothers with special events and corporate gifting but bring out-of-town employees to visit as a "must stop destination." Even TripAdvisor has sent people from near and far to Findlay just for Dietsch Brothers ice cream; the website ranked it among the top three in a list of the ten best ice cream shops in the United States for three consecutive years of the consumer-driven poll.

After over eighty years in business, Dietsch Brothers definitely deserves the rave reviews and loyal following in Findlay and beyond. As Erika fondly

Top: Dietsch Brothers 1962 original founders (*left to right*): brothers Chris "Bud," Don "Johnny," and Roy "Snitz." *Dietsch Brothers*.

Bottom: The Dietsch family carrying on their long legacy. *Dietsch Brothers*.

remembers the original building her founding family members worked hard to build, she recalls loving to come to "work" at the store, even as a little girl. Expanding her role as the operation itself expanded four times to its current footprint of twenty thousand square feet, Erika says it's "sometimes hard for me to wrap my head around all the growth. After our renovation projects were completed, we'd say, 'Gosh, how are we going to fill all this space' and about a year later, it's completely filled and we'd look around and start thinking about the next phase." Summing up her family's mutual commitment to Findlay, she adds, "While we might have several wholesale accounts that sell our chocolates (no ice cream) mainly in Northwest Ohio, the family doesn't have immediate plans to expand or open up stores outside of Findlay. With the size of our production areas, we're in a comfortable spot. The journey has been incredible and we're blessed to be a part of this community and to have such wonderful customers."

VELVET ICE CREAM

https://www.velveticecream.com/

It took a sweet tooth and a steel industry injury to start Joseph Dager down the path toward ice cream when, after relocating to Cleveland from Lebanon (the Middle Eastern country, not the Ohio town), he visited relatives in Utica and fell in love with the small-town feel. Four generations later, the Dager family continues his legacy, making an indelible mark on the area and bringing tourists from around as well as outside of the state to visit Ye Olde Mill.

According to the current Velvet president, Luconda Dager, her great-grandfather got his start in the basement of his cousin's confectionary, located on Main Street, where, as a self-made engineer, he started making the all-American dessert to rave reviews, eventually selling it to, first, a restaurant down the street, then to those within a five-mile radius. The business grew and was passed along to Luconda's grandfather, who, in the 1950s, partnered with the Kroger Company to abolish a previous ordinance that prohibited the sale of products made outside of Franklin County (Velvet is located in Licking County) to Kroger stores. After the court ruled in its favor, Velvet was able to sell not only to Kroger but also Big Bear and other independent grocers throughout Ohio and surrounding states, changing the trajectory of the business and positioning it for long-term growth into the third and fourth generations—and beyond.

Left: First Velvet distribution center opened in Bucyrus, Ohio, delivering ice cream in refrigerated trucks, 1937. *Velvet Ice Cream.*

Below: Community members enjoying the opening of Ye Olde Mill to the public, 1970. *Velvet Ice Cream.*

Another major milestone in Velvet's history is the opening of Ye Olde Mill in the 1970s. While not many plants invite consumers into their facilities, Velvet has become a destination for consumers, whether they're traveling to Amish country, Denison University, the Works in nearby Newark, one of Utica's orchards or simply taking a day trip for delicious ice cream. In fact, the crowds grew so much that while the shop originally only offered ice cream, a menu was added to include soups, salads and sandwiches (favorites are the reuben and the Buckeye Trail Bologna). But the nearly 160,000 guests each year know that the generous-sized dips of iconic Velvet flavors like Buckeye Classic, a peanut butter base with a thick swirl of Mackinac Island fudge and whole mini buckeye candies, or seasonal specials, such as Peaches and Cream, Apple Cobbler, Pumpkin Pie and Peppermint Stick, are still the star attractions. Nostalgic classics, such as Raspberry Fudge Cordial and a double down on Butter Pecan and Cashew, complement the offering of five types of vanilla: Original, Olde Tyme (similar to a French vanilla), Homemade Vanilla (more of a cooked flavor), Vanilla Bean and Vanilla Lovers Trio (a Neapolitan-style combination of Original, Olde Tyme and Vanilla Bean that gives back a portion of sales to breast cancer). Luconda herself loves any and all things chocolate, so the Double Dark Fudge is her purist pick.

With twenty-eight acres of beautiful parkland surrounding Ye Olde Mill, summer weekends are perfect for events, such as music and craft shows, especially during July, National Ice Cream Month. But the biggest event of the year kicks off the summer in style: the Utica Sertoma Ice Cream Festival, held annually on Memorial Day weekend. The three-day event features festival fun and raises over $65,000 for the international Sertoma Club by bringing in roughly forty thousand people. Ice cream is the "cherry on top" of a six-hundred-car Hot Rod Show and an ice cream–eating contest (the current record is eighteen pints in ten minutes).

In addition to the local Sertoma Club, Velvet has partnerships with Pelontonia (Luconda herself has ridden in the charity bike race multiple times) and the Stefanie Spielman Foundation (the Vanilla Lovers Trio has featured Spielman and three-time survivor Tatla Dager on the carton), as well as smaller groups, such as Hope Hollow, which assists cancer patients transitioning between hospital and home. "Past generations were givers," says Luconda, "and we're still very focused on community."

That commitment extends to the company's staff of nearly two thousand between the Utica facility and eight other branches throughout Ohio, Indiana and Kentucky, many of whom have been there between twenty

The summer months bring community together to celebrate ice cream. *Velvet Ice Cream.*

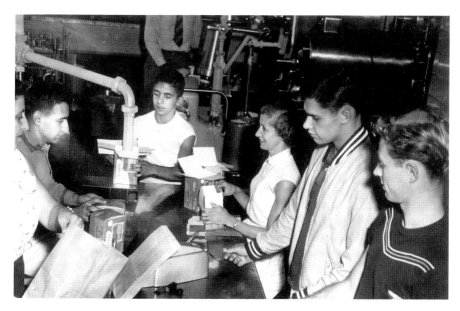

Mike Dager, working the filler, learning the business as a teen in the 1950s. *Velvet Ice Cream.*

and forty years. "It's like an extended family," according to Luconda, "and they're introducing the next generation." Similarly, there's already a fifth generation of Dagers working in the business, including Luconda's daughter Lauren and nephew Riley (the son of her sister Joanne, the current vice president overseeing Velvet's Ye Olde Mill and food service division), learning the ropes during summers off from high school and college. And there's even a three-page document called the "Dager Family Code of Ethics" that was written to guide them. After all, 3 percent or less of family businesses make it into the fourth generation, but even as both Luconda and Joanne ventured outside to start their careers, the sweet lull of ice cream—and family—brought them back.

From that very first hand-cranked gallon of vanilla made by Joseph Dager in 1914 to the more than 5 million gallons distributed yearly by the company today, family has and will continue to be at the center of operations at

Production supervisors ensuring all three-gallon tubs are filled, sealed and ready to be shipped out to parlor customers. *Velvet Ice Cream.*

Velvet has something for everyone, with a complete line of premium ice cream, novelties, sherbet and seasonal favorites. *Velvet Ice Cream.*

Velvet. Even as growth east of the Mississippi means partnerships with regional manufacturers, both sales and research and development will remain in Utica at Velvet headquarters. Says Luconda of the company's 107 years of consistency and each generation's impact on the Velvet legacy, "There are characteristics needed to survive in this industry; with so many manufacturers, especially in Ohio, one must be tenacious, have perseverance, stay fresh and relevant. Each generation brings personality and culture. We have never compromised our recipes, traditions or values because they are what make Velvet."

What else makes Velvet? Its signature, namesake, velvety texture. Because according to Joe Dager, Luconda's father, "All ice creams are good; some are just better than others."

Inside Scoop: A Festival Flavor

In 2014, Velvet made a flavor to celebrate the fortieth anniversary of the festival: a cinnamon ice cream base with pieces of fried funnel cake dough, aptly named Elephant Ear.

UTICA SERTOMA ICE CREAM FESTIVAL

Held Annually on Memorial Day Weekend (Saturday/Sunday/Monday)
https://sertomaicecreamfestival.com/

One of the oldest service clubs in America, Sertoma Inc. (formerly Sertoma International) was founded in 1912, right around the time Joseph Dager started making ice cream. The Sertoma name is an acronym for "Service to Mankind," and the group's main focus is hearing and speech health across the United States and Canada. The Utica chapter works with local school programs in both the Northridge and North Fork Districts, as well as with Little League Baseball and the Utica Fire and EMS Departments.

What started as a small event and partnership between the Sertoma Club and Velvet Ice Cream in 1974 has grown exponentially, says Bob Curtis, who has been involved since the beginning. "We started small, with a basic army tent," recalls Bob. "Now it's hard to tell how many people actually pass through because the parking lot is crammed full and the cars are packed."

Charging just five dollars per parked car, the festival features family-focused activities that are free of charge upon entry and include classics such as balloon toss, plank races and a kiddie tractor pull. Live music, a car show and crafts round out the entertainment, in addition to more than ninety artisans and food vendors.

Bookending the event, a parade through the village of Utica (a mile north of the Velvet Ice Cream/Energy Cooperative festival grounds) kicks things off on Saturday morning, while Monday afternoon's ice cream eating contest is the big eater's showdown showcase (smaller versions, which anyone can enter, are held each day).

"We're there for the people," says Bob, and the people are there for the ice cream, with over seventy-five thousand scoops estimated sold over the course of the long weekend. "There's a little bit of everything for everyone."

YOUNG'S JERSEY DAIRY

https://youngsdairy.com/

A dairy farm turned destination, Young's Jersey Dairy draws generational crowds excited to pet the cows (and goats!), play games like Udders & Putters (miniature golf) and eat ice cream—lots and lots of ice cream. While the property has been in the family since 1869, it wasn't until the late 1950s that Young's added its first retail store to the original family farm. Since then, the operation has grown from a simple roadside farmers market to an entertaining experience for all ages.

In the early days, the Young family sold milk from their cows, eventually bringing in meats and cheeses to complement the offering. The operation expanded in 1968, when the first part of the Dairy Store was built, and a nearby Dayton dairy, Moeller's, offered to private label ice cream to continue the product expansion. When that partner operation closed in 1978, Young's transitioned its ice cream production to Columbus, working with Borden's but struggled to grow its flavor offering during this relationship.

From its days as a dairy farm to a family-friendly destination, Young's retains its beauty. *John Young.*

So, in 1981, third-generation Dan Young, now CEO and chief ice cream dipper, worked with the Ohio State University to learn about ice cream making, purchased a single-batch freezer, started with quality ingredients and began making ice cream five gallons at a time. After that first summer, when the machine ran twenty hours a day, seven days a week, Dan and his cousin Ben Young (now Young's HR director) decided to get a second machine in 1982, which was able to make ten gallons at a time. Almost forty years later, in 2021, Young's production was roughly seventy thousand gallons, all made on-site (and 95 percent of it sold there, too).

With control of production, Dan and Ben were able to experiment and grow their offering from twenty to forty flavors (thirty during the winter season) and add between two and five new flavors each year. One of the first flavors the pair came up with is still Dan's personal favorite: Chocolate Fudge Brownie. The two were looking around the on-site bakery at what was available when they came up with the idea, now a menu staple. Other loyalist favorites are Butter Pecan, Black Walnut and Black Raspberry, while the best-selling kids' flavor is a bright-blue-hued Cotton Candy.

But the top spot for customers actually goes to a flavor Dan originally said "would never sell." Back in the mid-1980s, a staffer originally had the idea for a flavor Dan thought was too close to menu staple cookies and cream. Dan recalls this young lady, Jenny, reminding—almost pestering—him weekly about her concept, to which he responded, "Who is going to buy ice cream with raw cookie dough in it?" But they already had a bakery making cookies, so they had the dough, and he finally made a small batch. "It sold like crazy," he says, "and it caused me to stop, think and slow down. It's why I love small trials, and why I now tell all of our employees, 'Don't take no for an answer; figure out a way to get a yes.'"

Being the Buckeye State, there's of course a love of all things chocolate peanut butter, and the flavor is a top feature in treats like the Double Buckeye Sundae and the Buckeye Bull Shake. But Young's shares allegiance with more than just the Ohio State University, with both nearby University of Dayton and Wright State campuses using their ice cream and cheese and a flavor made especially for Miami University in Oxford's alumni weekend: Tuffy's Toasted Roll, a custom combination featuring the school diner's signature buttered, toasted cinnamon roll.

Beyond the sweets, Young's has delicious eats, one of which Dan says has nearly overcome the ice cream as the main motivation for visitors. Using some of the sixty to seventy thousand pounds of cheese made on-site, Young's deep-fried, breaded cheddar cheese curds are the number one side

With rides, slides and goats who are always up for meeting new friends, Young's is fun for the whole family. *John Young*

choice in the on-site restaurant, selling more than French fries. "Ten years ago, people associated us with ice cream and goats," says Dan. "Now it's cheese curds, goats and the ice cream's good too."

Speaking of goats, Young's doesn't milk theirs; they're simply there to have fun and socialize with guests, as they're a bit more interactive than the cows. Since the early 1990s, Young's has focused on adding elements that allow visitors to make a full day out of the experience, from two eighteen-hole miniature golf courses to a batting cage, driving range, mascot Cowvin's Fast Slide, a Kiddie Corral featuring tiny tractors, a corn pit and hay bales for the toddler set and Moovers & Shakers, a barrel passenger train that travels around the farm. The newest addition to Young's is a brand-new Dairy Store, opened in the fall of 2021, bringing more seating and parking and designed so visitors can watch both the ice cream and cheese being made.

With all of this excitement, it's easy to see why Dan says the first six words of Young's mission statement, created with Ben after they attended a Disney hospitality class, are "We create fun for our customers." And fun it sure is, especially during events like the Annual Wool Gathering (one of the largest wool shows east of the Mississippi, which celebrated 25 years in 2021) and Young's Birthday Celebration, which, in 2022, will celebrate 153 years of the family farm. From company picnics to school tours, Easter egg hunts to Independence Day celebrations (actually a full week of family value offerings), a pumpkin patch and a Christmas tree farm, there's always something going on at Young's.

"I've dipped a lot of ice cream in my career," Dan says as he sums up the operation, "and people are predisposed to be happy when you're giving them an ice cream cone. Some want mint chocolate chip and *only* mint chocolate chip. Some want to try it all and have trouble making a decision. There are no bad decisions; it's ice cream."

TOM'S ICE CREAM BOWL

https://www.tomsicecreambowl.com/

In over forty-four years, Joe Baker estimates he has made 798,000 gallons of ice cream at Tom's Ice Cream Bowl. But, the owner since 2019 demurs, that's only about 45 percent of all of the ice cream ever made in Zanesville by the long lineage of the Hemmer family since his great-grandfather Frank Edward (also known as F.E.) started the family business in 1887.

Joe speculates that the original Hemmer Ice Cream Company—the first commercial ice cream sales business in Zanesville and eventually the second largest in southeastern Ohio—made thirty times the amount of ice cream that Tom's Ice Cream Bowl has. But that business was sold by one of F.E.'s sons, Walter, after three of his four brothers who had worked in the business passed away; Walter accepted a job with the new owner, Borden, in California. It was F.E.'s grandson Jack Hemmer who, in 1948, partnered with his cousin Tom Mirgon, opening a small shop on Linden Avenue and leveraging the familial history in naming the place Jack Hemmer Ice Cream. As boys, the pair had worked selling novelties for their grandpa and great-grandpa, learning the inner workings of the ice cream operation, which they would build on to create their own legacy.

Tom's Ice Cream Bowl today. *Tom's Ice Cream Bowl.*

The first few years of the business went well; it quickly outgrew the first location and moved, in 1950, to its current spot at the intersection of McIntire and Maple Avenues. In 1953, Tom left his original career with the Pure Oil Company and bought out Jack's interest, though he waited a few more years to change the name to Tom's Ice Cream Bowl in 1957. Filling the hole left by the original Hemmer company's departure, the new business found great success in the community, owing in large part to Tom's dedication to quality and generosity, seen directly in the portion sizes of the restaurant's signature sundaes (served in soup bowls, including the banana split, forgoing its typical boat at Tom's). Customers also became stalwarts because of the personalized service of Tom's employees, one of whom, manager Bill Sullivan, would buy the business upon Tom's retirement in 1984.

At the time only eighteen years old, but having worked in the business for nearly seven years already, Joe (a cousin to Jack on his father's side, though not related to Tom) continued to work in the business, supporting Bill by making 95 percent of the ice cream (if Joe was on vacation, Bill might occasionally need to make a batch of fast-selling vanilla). Then, in 2019,

Bill sold the business to Joe, who also purchased his grandfather's company name in 2000, owning the rights to both the Hemmer Ice Cream Company and its subsidiary, Tom's Ice Cream Bowl.

Though Joe has no plans to change the classic atmosphere, he's already made some major upgrades, including remodeling the back-of-the-house kitchen and back room, installing new flooring and a patio, improving the parking lot and adding a party building. But the star of the show is always the ice cream, which he's perfected over the years. "I think I've changed everything except the Vanilla," says Joe. "The Peach took three tries to get to where it is now."

Taking inspiration from his travels, including ice cream trade shows and trips to his happy place—Disneyland, the "happiest place on Earth"—Joe aligns with a Walt Disney ethos: "How do we plus it?" It's under this guidance that Joe has invented favorites like the Chocolate Caramel Marshmallow Fudge, Red Raspberry Grand and Cherry Cordial, originally a riff on White House Cherry (a cherry vanilla flavor preferred by President Andrew Jackson and served at the property for which it is named). Working with trusted suppliers, Joe sought out input for the flavor, but "plussed it" by combining not only three chocolate sources but three cherry ingredients, with both mixed into the base ice cream as well as front and center in ribbons and chunks throughout. "No one's crazy enough to do it this way," says Joe, "but it's the best. No one else's tastes like mine." In addition to the seasonal favorite, other specials include Pumpkin and Caramel Apple Strudel for Thanksgiving and holiday features, such as Peppermint Stick, Rum Raisin and Egg Nog. Old-fashioned classics Butter Pecan and Maple Nut share space on the Standards menu alongside hip newcomers Chocolate Chip Cookie Dough and Oreo (made with the Double Stuf variation, crushed by hand).

Of course, there's chocolate, strawberry and mint chocolate chip, too, but best-selling vanilla serves as the base for Tom's namesake sundaes. From Tin Roof to Buckeye, Brownie or Banana Caramel, you really can't go wrong. But the Black and White might be the ultimate "plussed up" classic, featuring three large dips of vanilla ice cream, chocolate syrup and—wait for it—marshmallows!

To accompany all that sweet, Tom's offers an ample savory menu of sandwiches, soups and sides, including the house recipe Hot Virginia Ham, as well as a breakfast menu for when you need your ice cream before noon (pro tip: pancakes and French toast can be topped with your favorite flavor). Comfort foods also "plussed up" the menu in 2020, when Tom's brought

Sprinkle sundae topped with chocolate sauce, always a classic. *Johnson's Real Ice Cream.*

Serving up scoops around town thanks, to the Johnson's ice cream truck. *Johnson's Real Ice Cream.*

Above: Keeping it classic—
Buckeye Classic, that is—at
Velvet. *Velvet Ice Cream.*

Left: The milkshake makes
the meal at Velvet's Ye Olde
Mill. *Velvet Ice Cream.*

Top: Looks like Cookie
Monster got ahold of the
Handel's. *Handel's Ice Cream.*

Bottom: Handel's signature
Graham Central Station.
Handel's Ice Cream.

Even Cowvin gets in on the big slide action at Young's. *Young's Jersey Dairy*.

Doubling down on Ohio's favorite pairing—peanut butter and chocolate—because the only thing that beats a buckeye sundae is a Double Buckeye Sundae. *Young's Jersey Dairy*.

Top: A classic, upgraded: Strawberry Serenity at Simply Rolled. *Simply Rolled.*

Bottom: Ice cream fusion comes to life in the form of a Cotton Candy Burrito at Simply Rolled. *Simply Rolled.*

Above: Pints (and sauces) make a party Graeter! *Graeter's.*

Left: A freezer full of color and flavor from Jeni's Splendid Ice Creams. *Jeni's Splendid Ice Creams.*

Above: Jeni's signature
Salty Caramel in the
making. *Jeni's Splendid
Ice Creams.*

Left: A finished
pint of fire-toasted
sugar, sea salt and
vanilla becomes
Jeni's signature Salty
Caramel. *Jeni's Splendid
Ice Creams.*

Miss King Kone approves of the double dip of mint chocolate chip. *Navatsyk Photography*.

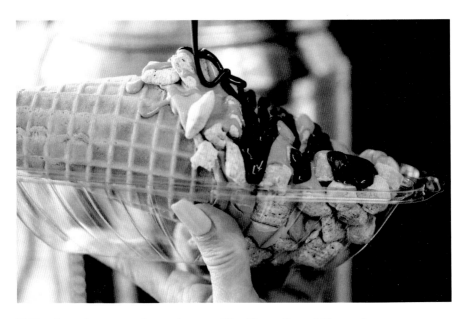

Taking that twist up a notch—or three—at King Kone. *Navatsyk Photography*.

Above: Sprinkles squeeze out of a King Kone ice cream sandwich. *Navatsyk Photography*.

Left: Cookie Butter, as a shake or by the pint— it's all good at Ritzy's. *Graydon Webb*.

Sprinkled with love, from Little Ladies. *Phil Navatsyk.*

A trio of signature sundaes for the three Little Ladies who inspired the brand. *Phil Navatsyk.*

Above: Another team tribute: CRMD's creation for the Columbus Crew soccer team, in black and a brightly hued burst of yellow. *Dakota Dean, @dakotadeanvisualmedia.*

Left: A colorful tower of taste and texture at CRMD. *CRMD.*

Is it just me, or is the chair even eyeing that classic combo of hot fudge and caramel on a Sweet Moses sundae? *Sweet Moses, Ltd.*

Pierre's Spirit of America ice cream on the packaging line. *Pierre's Ice Cream Company.*

Above: Whipty-Do's signature blueberry ice cream, a fan favorite taste of the nearby amusement park. *Whipty-Do.*

Left: Tom's take on a banana split, served vertically. *Tom's Ice Cream Bowl.*

Local artist Kathy Anderson's painting of Whit's flagship in downtown Granville. *Whit's Frozen Custard, Kathy Anderson.*

"A glorious full moon rises over the Zip Dip ice cream shop on a warm summer night in Green Township, Ohio. The classic, and original, 1950s neon of a cone and lightning bolt is a photographer's dream." *Terrence Huge.*

Pretty in pink and full of old-fashioned charm, both sides of Aglamesis Bros. delight. *Aglamesis Brothers*.

This page: Mason's ube ice cream two ways: in a pandan coconut egg waffle (*top*) or paired with local business Honeypot Bakes' ube macaron for a double dose of color and flavor (*left*). *Jesse Mason*.

in beef or chicken noodles, pot roast and meatloaf during the pandemic alongside a DoorDash delivery option.

But back to the sugar, shall we? Don't miss Tom's to-go offering of candy and nuts (it's right there under the name on the sign, after all). Joe says they'll sell eleven and a half tons of candy and six tons of nuts at Christmastime, all sourced directly from Heggy's Chocolates in Canton. Valentine's Day and Easter also bring in special chocolates, like hearts and cream-filled eggs.

Nearly unchanged, albeit "plussed up" quite a bit, in over seventy years, Tom's Ice Cream Bowl serves up 1950s diner nostalgia with every super-sized sundae as Joe Baker carries on the revived family legacy for generations of Zanesville ice cream lovers.

Inside Scoop: A Better Bowl (and an Astronaut's Inspiration)

When Jack and Tom opened Jack Hemmer's Ice Cream in 1948, traditional banana boats were expensive and, being glass, breakable. Long a center for pottery manufacturing, Zanesville at the time was known as the "Clay City," with potteries littered all over the county. Looking around to see what else he might serve a banana split in, Tom went out and found a nice little white bowl, serving them vertically.

At the time, a college student at Muskingum University in New Concord, future astronaut and senator John Glenn, often visited the shop, ordering a Black and White sundae. As Joe recalls from meeting both John and his wife, Annie, on several occasions, it was John who said his "favorite place to get ice cream was a little place called Tom's where he can get three

A classic sundae in Tom's namesake bowl. *Tom's Ice Cream Bowl.*

scoops in a soup bowl." Hence, when he took on full ownership, Tom drew upon this distinction, originally driven by cost effectiveness but now a unique namesake, changing the business's name to Tom's Ice Cream Bowl.

A tray full of John Glenn's favorite sundaes, the Black and White. *Tom's Ice Cream Bowl.*

JOHNSON'S REAL ICE CREAM

https://johnsonsrealicecream.com/

Imagine coming into a 1940s grocery store and requesting your favorite ice cream flavor, only to have it made especially for you and ready for pickup the very next day. In Bexley, a suburb of Columbus, this reality was the start of Johnson's Real Ice Cream.

While running the meat processing plant next door to the supermarket, Robert Johnson and his son-in-law James Wilcoxon realized that they had extra space in the freezers they were using to store meat. They came up with the idea to purchase a small ice cream machine and store the flavors in the freezers. The ice cream portion of their business grew until 1950, when they took the same ice cream machine and moved it back to their building, opening the first Johnson's storefront on September 1 as a ten-by-ten-foot walkup window only, with the rest of the building dedicated to production.

THE OHIO STATE FAIR BUTTER COW—AND CONE

If any further proof was needed of Ohio's long history as a dairy state, one might look to the annual state fair, at which the Dairy Processors of Ohio, in coordination with the Ohio State University, have been sponsoring butter-sculpting contests since the early 1900s.

While much of the competition's legacy is credited to the "butter cow"—a tradition first featured in 1903 (sculpted by A.T. Shelton & Company, distributors of Sunbury Co-Operative Creamery butter) and now an annual staple at the event—the Dairy Products Building, built in the 1920s, has hosted an exhibit featuring other sculptures alongside the cow (and its calf) since the 1960s, when the American Dairy Association Mideast took over sponsorship.

In 1994, to celebrate the ninetieth anniversary of the ice cream cone, longtime lead butter sculptor Paul Brooke, a Cincinnati resident who professionally sculpted toy models for the Kenner Company and Hasbro, and his team created a seven-foot-tall ice cream cone out of butter, which he recalls as one of his favorite sculptures—in addition to the cows, of course.

Seventy-one years later, 90 percent of Johnson's production is still made on-site, and the recipes for many of its flavors haven't changed much either. The family still relies on a single copy of an old paper notebook, handwritten three and four generations ago, with classics like vanilla; seasonal specials, such as peach; and fan favorites, including black licorice (still a request from loyal customers, though the signature ingredient can no longer be sourced).

In the 1970s, second-generation owner Jim Wilcoxon Jr. took over the business and expanded the operation to include a deli-style offering to support year-round operations, enticing people to dine in and order a meal with their ice cream. Jim Jr.'s son Matt got his start in the family business early. When he was around eleven or twelve, his grandma would put him on the bus in Reynoldsburg, which dropped him off right at the shop to join his dad and grandpa. There, he helped clean tables and wipe windows and eventually learned the steps to making homemade ice cream.

This page, top: The first and still standing location of Johnson's in Bexley. *Johnson's Real Ice Cream.*

This page, bottom: Street view of Johnson's Super Market. *Johnson's Real Ice Cream.*

Opposite: Behind the scenes at Johnson's. *Johnson's Real Ice Cream.*

Matt recalls his dad pulling fresh ice cream off the machine to try and his grandpa, who gave him the moniker "Big Dipper," which still sticks today (Matt's younger brother Jeff, now the company's CFO, was known as the "Little Dipper"). His favorite flavor? "If you'd believe it, vanilla," says the fourth-generation owner. "When I travel and try other ice cream shops, I always get the vanilla. If you can do vanilla right, you can pretty much do any flavor."

Family values and traditional flavors are the hallmarks of Johnson's success, though the company does experiment, and one creation has become a customer favorite: Salty Caramel Chocolate Pretzel. Young customers often tend toward the eye-catching Blue Sky and Cotton Candy flavors, while fans of the Ohio State University (and lovers of the state's unofficial candy, named for its official tree) love the Buckeye Fever. Johnson's even takes the classic chocolate and peanut butter combination up a notch by making Ice Cream Buckeyes, hand-scooped peanut butter ice cream dipped in chocolate. And the family listens to its loyal customer base, with Matt recalling the time they removed Banana from the menu, leaving only Banana with Fudge. An anonymous customer left a notebook in the dining room, starting a petition that hundreds of people signed. "As an owner, sometimes you think you need to make a change, but people let you know when they want it back," says Matt.

Left: The recipe book passed down through the generations at Johnson's. *Johnson's Real Ice Cream.*

Below: Fourth-generation owner Matt Wilcoxon (*cutting ribbon*). *Johnson's Real Ice Cream.*

With over fifty flavors at its main location (sister shops in Dublin, opened in 2017, and New Albany, opened in 2019, offer the must-haves alongside a slightly smaller seasonal rotation), customers can truly find any flavor they're seeking, including dairy-free, vegan and no-sugar-added options. Sundaes, milkshakes, ice cream sandwiches and celebration cakes round out the lineup, with pints available to go as well as at grocers throughout the state.

Continued growth for the next generation has also meant becoming a part of the mobile scene, starting with a delivery cart in 2010, expanding in

Johnson's gone mobile with the addition of a fleet of ice cream trucks. *Johnson's Real Ice Cream.*

2015 with a converted cupcake trailer and adding a second truck in 2020. Johnson's was one of the first mobile ice cream offerings in Columbus, and customers and businesses alike were quick to take advantage of having Johnson's brought to them, hosting ice cream socials and having scoops, sundaes and shakes all made on-site for office parties, weddings and other events.

Big events in the company's calendar always include the Fourth of July in Bexley and the Columbus Food Truck Festival, held annually in August. A partnership with the children's charity A Kid Again, called Every Scoop Counts, gives donations from the sale of every single Johnson's pint to the organization; the A Kid Again/Every Scoop Counts logo is also featured on signature pints. And participation in the Ohio Ice Cream Trail makes Johnson's a destination for travelers throughout the state, who might even catch a glimpse of "Scoops," the company mascot.

The fourth generation looks to carry on what Johnson's Real Ice Cream has meant for generations: a family-focused, community-connected tradition of good-quality, homemade ice cream meant to scoop up smiles throughout

Pints and other packaging throughout the decades at Johnson's. *Johnson's Real Ice Cream.*

Pick your pint of Johnson's (this author is partial to PB Choco Tornado). *Johnson's Real Ice Cream.*

central Ohio. The key to a multigenerational family business, according to Matt, is that "each generation adapts, evolving to support the next, while sticking to the company's roots and what they do well." Great-Grandpa Johnson would indeed be proud of the family's evolution from small side project to today's trajectory of his namesake.

FOOD FAN FAVORITES

Johnson's is known for its namesake ice cream, but the Bexley location boasts a deli menu featuring soups and sandwiches that have developed nearly as loyal a following.

Here's a top three to eat before (or after) your ice cream.

- Reuben (most popular)
- Johnson's sub (Italian sub bun, American cheese, provolone cheese, Bavarian ham, sliced salami, onion, banana peppers and Italian dressing)
- Any of the made-fresh-daily egg/chicken/tuna salad options (also available as a melt)

WHIT'S FROZEN CUSTARD

https://whitscustard.com/

Two love stories form the beginnings of Whit's Frozen Custard—the first, that of Chuck and Lisa Whitman, founders and franchisors of the business; the second, that of their foundational love for ice cream, developed from each of their families' backgrounds in food service.

For his part, Chuck spent over twenty years calling on restaurants throughout the Midwest while working in his father's food service business. He was drawn specifically to the soft serve ice cream clients, eventually working in a dairy manufacturing plant while experimenting at home with ingredients to make his own, eventually focusing on frozen custard. On her end, Lisa, who grew up in her family's Dairy Queen stores around the Columbus area and who had a strong affinity for their ice cream, tasted the creaminess and flavor of Chuck's frozen custard, and a shared passion was born.

Bringing these influences together and bringing them back from Florida to Ohio in 2002, Chuck and Lisa searched for a small community in which to start their business, originally introducing frozen custard to the residents of Granville in March 2003. Not only did the opening come on the heels of one of the town's coldest winters, but the case for custard still had to be made, after all. Was it actually ice cream or not?

In fact, frozen custard is a premium ice cream product, said to have been made popular during the 1933 World's Fair in Chicago (though recipes date back as far

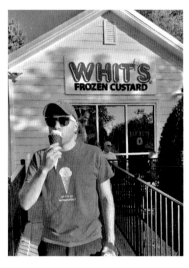

Whit's has a loyal local following (check out his T-shirt). *Whit's Frozen Custard.*

as the early 1900s, with commercial machines invented in the 1920s). The thicker, smoother, creamier product caught on quickly, and by 1940, frozen custard stands had opened across the Midwest and East Coast. While the recipe still starts with the same ingredients as it did back then—cream, eggs and sugar—three things differentiate custard from traditional ice cream: (1) a higher butterfat content, (2) a slower, more labor-intensive process that seeks to minimize air in the mix and (3) temperature (it's served at twenty-six degrees, ten degrees warmer than ice cream).

Whether they knew what it was or found the flavor experience to be a totally new taste, Ohioans loved the Whitman's creation—so much so that customers began approaching them with questions about franchising, something they hadn't quite considered. As soon as 2008, the first Whit's franchise opened in Lebanon, spurring growth quickly, first within Ohio and then beyond. Now spanning ten states, Whit's has seventy locations, thirty-two of which are in Ohio. Chuck and Lisa say that, though unplanned, one of their biggest business accomplishments is, "hands down, giving families an opportunity to get into their own business and be successful."

And while each location's autonomy allows it to reflect the local community that surrounds it (both in appearance as well as working with local bakeries for inclusions like doughnuts and cake), customers know that they're getting the high-quality recipe developed for Whit's delicious, fresh

Make mine a Whitser!
Tim Robison Creative.

frozen custard over forty years ago by the Whitman family. The custard is churned on-site every day in every shop—not in a factory—meaning scoops, quarts and pints are freshly hand packed. Signature flavors, such as Butter Pecan, Almond Joy and Buckeye, a nod to the brand's central Ohio home base, share the menu in a rotation as flavor of the week (or day, in some locations), while classic vanilla and chocolate are always available. "Despite having over 350 flavors, our Vanilla is still our most popular," say Chuck and Lisa. "Made with quality cream, eggs and sugar and made fresh throughout the day every day, the simple goodness of our Vanilla stands out on its own as a customer favorite." Their favorite? "The Whitser of course!" They add, "It is our favorite item because essentially, a Whitser allows you to create your own flavor using our premium frozen custard and a variety of toppings. You can create a different flavor every time you visit a Whit's."

Overwhelmed by topping options (from fruits to candies, nuts to bites, there's lots to choose)? Get inspired by one of the specialties, mixed for a Whitser or topped for a sundae: choices like Buckeye Madness, Hawaiian Lu'au or the O'Henry George, named after the couple's son, who now works on the business alongside sister Kaylyn. This focus on family carries through each Whit's location, family-owned and committed to both the community and the custard. Meeting trends in consumer dietary preferences, most

A flavorful lineup of signatures and specials. *Jacob Sapp.*

Whit's locations now offer one or two vegan products, either a coconut milk base or a gluten-free oat milk base, with location information available online.

Other features include the Whittie, custard sandwiched between two cookies; the Whit Stick, vanilla custard dipped in chocolate and served on a stick (topped with nuts for a Nutty Whit); and custard Floats, such as the Dreamsicle, vanilla custard mixed with orange soda, or the Black Cow, vanilla custard mixed with root beer and a shot of chocolate syrup. For the kiddos, creations like the Dirty Worm, Fish Bait and Happy Sundae are as fun to order as they are to eat. Milkshakes and malts round out the menu, while custard cakes are available for carryout celebrations, both grab-and-go and special order.

Continuing on its growth trajectory, Chuck and Lisa believe that Whit's will continue to open locations throughout various regions of the United States, saying, "The future of ice cream will always be strong because everyone treats or rewards themselves to an ice cream cone." And so the love story continues for the Whitmans, the Whit's families and those who love their ice cream (ahem, frozen custard).

PIERRE'S

https://pierres.com/

When Alexander "Pierre" Basset opened his namesake shop's doors in 1932 at what was then a chic corner of East Eighty-Second Street and Euclid Avenue in Cleveland, he likely couldn't have dreamed of the facility that still bears his name ninety years later, just one mile west, holding 36 million scoops of gourmet ice cream. But that reality is alive and well at East Sixth Street, where Shelley Roth, Pierre's president since 1991, oversees the continuation of a two-family, two-generation legacy.

Shelley's father, Sol Roth, the child of an immigrant family, owned the Royal Ice Cream Company, a small ice cream manufacturing business that

Pierre's Ice Cream Shoppe, 1930s–40s. *Pierre's Ice Cream Company.*

Pierre's factory, 1940s. *Pierre's Ice Cream Company.*

Pierre's delivery truck, 1960s–70s. *Pierre's Ice Cream Company.*

shared space with Pierre's after the company's move to Hough Avenue in 1960. From its early days of selling ice cream by the cone, cup and hand-packed pint, Pierre's had expanded, first moving to St. Clair Avenue, then to East Sixtieth Street and Hough Avenue. After Royal acquired Pierre's and maintained its brand and special recipes (original flavors included French vanilla, Swiss chocolate and strawberry), it proceeded to purchase the Harwill Ice Cream Company (East Sixty-Fifth Street and Carnegie Avenue) in 1967. Joining her father in the 1980s, Shelley purchased the company from him in 1991 and oversaw the move to the current company headquarters in 1995, as well as the opening of a thirty-five-thousand-square-foot state-of-the-art-factory in 2011.

Committed to quality and food safety, Pierre's was one of the first ice cream producers in the country to achieve SQF Level 3 certification, the industry's highest achievable level (the company recertifies annually). It's also committed to Cleveland, serving as an anchor in the MidTown community since the early 1990s, reinvesting in the revitalization of the surrounding area and serving as a model for areas known as "brownfield sites," which require extensive environmental remediation. Creating a path for future companies to invest in communities with similar challenges, Pierre's modern facilities are a shining example of how private and public enterprise can collaborate to rehabilitate urban industrial areas. Designed for efficiency and sustainability, the facility even uses the hot and cold air used in the ice cream–making process to heat and cool the building and collects its waste, sending it to be converted into energy.

Pierre's is also committed to its people; some staff have been with the company for anywhere between fifteen, twenty-five and even thirty-five years. Family-owned and focused on encouraging employee growth, Pierre's prides itself on providing premium products in an environment that values exceeding expectations. Shelley carries on the strength of the company culture Sol built around him, cultivating a team of ice cream makers devoted to delicious research and development, including selecting the best fruits, nuts, candy, cookie chunks and dough pieces, chocolate chips and thick fudges and peanut butter swirls.

It's those premium inclusions that make the flavors Pierre's has developed a loyal fan base on. From Pumpkin Pie to Peppermint Stick (a most-anticipated seasonal limited edition offering, sold from September through the winter holidays but often requested starting in the summer), Coconut

Pierre's factory, 1980s. *Pierre's Ice Cream Company.*

Pierre's factory, 2000s. *Pierre's Ice Cream Company.*

Pineapple to Spirit of America (a patriotic take on Neapolitan, featuring Pierre's strawberry, vanilla and blueberry ice creams), Pierre's lineup features over fifty flavors. Within that wide array, Pierre's assortment of vanillas shines, with an exceptional take on French Vanilla, an original that's been around since the very beginning, distinguished by the use of pasteurized egg yolks to enhance its rich, creamy taste and texture. Equally loved are Classic Vanilla and Vanilla Bean, with all three ranked among the top of Pierre's fan favorites. Innovating with the times, Pierre's also offers lactose-free, no-sugar-added, reduced-fat and light ice creams, all packaged in updated versions of Pierre's original, signature striped design.

"It's always exciting to see each new generation rediscover, love and support Pierre's as much as their own families did while they were growing up," says Shelley. "Our heritage means a lot to us and we've been within three miles of our original location, right in the heart of Cleveland, since 1932."

Inside Scoop: An Anchor with a Sweet Tooth

While working in Cleveland in the 1980s, Al Roker produced a segment about Pierre's for WKYC Channel 3 that won an Emmy award.

Chapter 3

FAMOUS FLAVORS

*I*cons in their own right, many scoop shops have flavors so famous they've cultivated their own following. Among these are the Cone's Orange Vanilla Swirl (so synonymous, the company even bought a building to match the offering), Ritzy's award-winning 1983 Richest Chocolate and Hartzler Family Dairy's aptly named Heifer Trails, a take on the state's favorite combination of peanut butter and chocolate.

Pushing flavor profiles even further are the inventive and influential tastes of Jeni's Splendid Ice Creams's Salty Caramel, Mason's Ube and CRMD's Viet Coffee. Bringing Ohio into the future of what's possible with new takes on a most familiar frozen treat, these purveyors put taste front and center—perhaps unexpected but most definitely delicious.

THE CONE

https://thecone.com/

You simply can't miss the giant orange and vanilla soft serve cone at the intersection of Tylersville and Cincinnati Dayton Roads in West Chester, as its iconic shape and color entice you to drive in (or thru, as they offer one, if that's more your speed) and taste a bit of classic Creamsicle nostalgia.

Owner Keith Wren recalls opening in 1995 after purchasing the building from a closed operation in Florida, saying, "When we were first building

Happy customers every time at the Cone. *The Cone.*

the Cone we had a lot of people say we would never make it because our location is at the end of a business district." Now, over twenty-five years later, he says, "We are one of the busiest single store locations in the area."

Keith credits much of the Cone's success to his late father, original business partner and inspiration, Kenneth Wren, who got the family into the ice cream business in 1973 with his wife, Louella. The pair opened K&W Creamy Whip in the Lockland-Reading area, devoting long hours to developing a loyal customer following while getting their young family in on the action early (Keith himself started around age fourteen, younger brother Kyle at age twelve and sister Tricia almost from birth, sleeping in an empty cone box when brought to the store as a baby). Ken's original inspiration was his own first job: while he was working in a deli down the street from where his sister worked at the local dairy bar, she would ask him to come over and pour the ice cream into the machines because the five-gallon metal containers were too heavy for her. At just fifteen, his dream of owning his own ice cream store was born.

With the same recipe for Orange and Vanilla Swirl that his parents opened with in 1973, the Cone continues the family legacy, and is still the number one seller. Over the years, Keith has added new offerings, with a focus on real ingredients, such as Cone-made strawberry ice cream with fresh strawberries and no artificial flavor. All of the soft serve ice creams are egg free, soy free and gluten free, and there are peanut-safe, dairy-free and sugar-free options, such as sherbets, Italian ices and yogurts. Sundaes, shakes, sodas and slushes round out the menu, alongside parfaits, banana boats and "Wizzards," the Cone's blended treat that offers seasonal and monthly specials. Non–ice cream offerings include edible raw cookie dough, available by the scoop, with or without ice cream and even in its own "boat," as well as thirty flavors of Hawaiian shave ice, dairy free and made daily on-site with all-natural flavors (the Cone purchased Hawaiian Five-OH in 2020 and now operates three independent mobile units under that banner).

Keith strays from the old-fashioned Creamsicle taste of the Cone's signature Orange and Vanilla Swirl only for the company's peanut butter offerings, another made-daily flavor featuring the Cone's homemade gourmet peanut butter sauce. It's this dedication to making or enhancing almost all of its soft serve flavors with the actual product—Cone-made peach and melon are summer staples, while pumpkin is a fan favorite come fall— that gives the Cone its bespoke taste. Keith works with suppliers specifically for ingredients, such as produce from Garver Farm (to whom the Cone, in turn, supplies ice cream), a vanilla made especially for the Cone by Lockhead Vanillas and homemade doughnuts from Neiderman Farms for a specialty sundae offered during Doughnut Days.

The menu isn't the only thing that has expanded over the years, as the family added on to the physical space in 2005 and again in 2009, building out a game room with ten-plus pinball, arcade and redemption-type games, as well as an enclosed outdoor area to house "Kiddie Land," a dozen coin-operated ride-on machines for the younger set. But Keith credits his father, again, with the most impactful expansion decision, the drive-thru, added in 2007. The double-lane drive-thru can hold thirty cars at one time, and a third lane opens for special events, allowing up to forty. During the height of the season, there are regularly six lanes of drive-thru traffic, and a carhop system, with waiters coming to the car to take and deliver orders, is used to keep orders flowing efficiently. The Cone added two additional lanes, for a total of eight, as the 2020 season started during the COVID-19 pandemic, giving the drive-thru and employees a true test—and they rose to the challenge.

After looking to expand operations to the mobile scene, the company found the perfect truck in Louisiana in 2005 and hit the scene after undergoing major renovations. In 2019, with two more mobile units added, the Cone hit the road for more than three hundred events. From St. Max's Festival to the Riverfest WEBN Fireworks and private gatherings, such as graduations and

The Cone's closing-day line as customers stock up for the off season. *The Cone.*

weddings, the mobile Cone is a hit throughout Butler County and beyond.

It's this great community that Keith credits with also bringing friends and relatives to the Cone when they visit the area, saying, "Our customers appreciate the fact that we are about quality and they support us heavily." He adds, "Many old dairies started in this part of Ohio—French Bauer, Meyer Dairy, Trauth—just to name a few," which makes residents especially fond of treats like ice cream.

The family dynasty continues with Keith's daughter, Tabitha "Tabby," who also started working at the Cone around age twelve. "I think the ice cream industry will grow especially with independent operators like us," says Keith, "as we share a passion to carry only the best." Voted exactly that (Cincinnati's best soft serve) by *Cincinnati Magazine*'s readers, as well as "One of the Top Ten Quirkiest Places to Visit in the U.S." by AOL.com, the Cone is sure to be an essential seasonal stop for many more generations to come.

Ritzy's

https://www.ritzyscolumbus.com/

When the chocolate ice cream is good enough to be ranked number one in America by *People* magazine, it's easy to imagine both the sorrow that loyalists of the original G.D. Ritzy's felt when it closed in 1991 and the joy that those same fans and a new crop of their descendants experienced when the new incarnation (dropping the "G.D.") opened in 2018.

Originally founded by former food and beverage executive Graydon D. Webb in 1981, the concept's original and current iterations both focus on bringing back a 1950s diner–style atmosphere, pairing crispy-edged smashed hamburgers with hand-cut shoestring-style fries—and, of course, that award-winning ice cream. Graydon got his start early when his family owned the Totem Dairy Bar in New Boston, then acquired a Stewart's Root Beer franchise and added a Kentucky Fried Chicken. While he was attending the Ohio State University, his father's business connections led him to meet Dave Thomas and subsequently join the first management team at Wendy's. After learning the ropes and rising to the position of vice president of franchise sales, he left in 1980 to go out on his own, opening Ritzy's.

The initial concept had great success, becoming publicly owned in just two years and growing to over one hundred locations by 1986. But the expansion proved too rapid, with the company retracting to just a few stores after its first decade and the last Columbus location closing in 1991. After a near-thirty-year hiatus, Graydon's sons Corey and Bryan and business partner Drew DeVilbiss sought to rebirth the concept, choosing a high-traffic location right on High Street in north Clintonville. It opened to long lines at both counters (ice cream has both a dedicated ordering counter and an exterior walk-up window), with fans excited for both the taste memory as well as the opportunity to introduce those who were trying it for the first time.

Whether you're inside or out, the menu board beckons with favorites old and new, from Philadelphia Style Vanilla to Butter Pecan Cashew, Cookie Butter and Coffee Break. Looking for that chocolate? It's aptly named "1983 Richest Chocolate," and its counterpart, the Chunky Dory Fudge, takes the decadence a step further, incorporating real pieces of Main Street Gourmet fudge brownies. Whether you make it a shake, a float or a simple scoop or double down with an ice cream sandwich, Graydon says each flavor is rich, refreshing and "oh so smooth," due to the limited incorporation of air used in the ice cream–making process.

Ranking the 30 finest flavors in the land

REGULAR

1. (tie) **VANILLA.** Toscanini's, Cambridge, Mass.

 BLUEBERRY. Great Midwestern, Iowa City, Iowa.

3. **VANILLA BEAN.** Chubby's of Tulsa.

4. **FRENCH VANILLA.** Bassetts, Philadelphia.

5. (tie) **BUTTER PECAN.** Guernsey Farms Dairy, Novi, Mich.

 CHOCOLATE CHIP WITH MOLASSES CHIP. University of Wisconsin, Madison.

7. **STRAWBERRY.** Bauder's Pharmacy, Des Moines.

8. **PRALINE PECAN.** Angel Food Ice Cream, Memphis.

9. **COFFEE.** Häagen-Dazs, Manhattan.

10. **VANILLA.** Bern's Steak House, Tampa, Fla.

CHOCOLATE

1. **G.D. RITZY'S,** Columbus, Ohio.

2. **HABER'S,** Miami.

3. **LEE'S,** Baltimore.

4. **GRAETER'S,** Cincinnati.

5. **DR. MIKE'S,** Bethel, Conn.

6. **GELÁRE,** Dallas.

7. **HOLY COW,** Odessa, Mo.

8. **GIFFORD'S,** Silver Spring, Md.

9. **LONDON CHOP HOUSE,** Detroit.

10. **BRAVO FONO,** Palo Alto.

EXOTICS

1. **COOKIES 'N CREAM.** United Dairy Farmers, Cincinnati.

2. **BANANA PUDDING.** Elliott's Old Fashioned Ice Cream, Statesville, N.C.

3. **DIVINE DECADENCE.** Mary B. Best Extravagant Ice Cream, Oakland.

4. **COCONUT MACADAMIA.** Dave's, Honolulu.

5. **GINGER CARDAMON.** 15th St. Grill, Tulsa.

6. **CHOCOLATE RASPBERRY TRUFFLE.** Via Dolce, L.A.

7. **CREOLE CREAM CHEESE.** Swensen's, New Orleans.

8. **TRUFFLE SUPREME.** Roberto's, Portland, Oreg.

9. **SHERRY EGGNOG.** Satsuma Tea Room, Nashville.

10. **CRÈME DE COCOA.** Herrell's Ice Cream, Cambridge, Mass.

I t's been around here for a long time, since 1700 in fact, but suddenly ice cream is on the tip of everyone's tongue. Boutiques proffering X-rated flavors and warm, off-the-griddle cones are springing up at every shopping mall, the theory being that if you can't quite afford that Mercedes or mink, you can splurge on a double-dip macadamia nut swirl with a designer pedigree.

With $2.7 billion wholesale at stake annually—which buys more than 15 quarts for every man, woman and child in the land—there's a rush to scoop the competition. The giant Borden company has snapped up nationwide supermarket distribution rights for Geláre, a fledgling San Diego concern with 15 franchises and an eye toward opening 30 more. Legendary Steve's of Somerville, Mass. has been bought by Integrated Resources, which plans to open 500 stores. And Himself, first owner Steve Herrell, has started franchising under his own last name.

Already successful folk a menting their careers by ch their own dream creams. P: professor Debora Phillips o University School of Medici Hobson's trendy sweet sho; Barbara and L.A., figuring th health could be had for $2 a as for $150 for an hour on th Says Philip Keeney, head o Science Department at Per and the nation's No. 1 ice cr

The panel at work: From left, Ahmad Rashad, Justin Henry, Krista Tesreau, Herb Wolff, Carol Robbins, Barry Beck, Tisha Ford, Stan Isaacs

Above: Ritzy's Richest Chocolate takes the top spot in *People* magazine, June 4, 1984. *Graydon Webb*.

Opposite: Ritzy's exterior at night. *Graydon Webb*.

"Our mix is from a family recipe dating back to the 1930s and processed in Ohio by one of the few dairies in the Midwest that can process without the addition of stabilizers, gums and other chemical compounds." He adds, "We thank Ohio Processors/Instantwhip for their commitment to quality." That same trait is the reason Graydon holds Graeter's over-one-hundred-year legacy and Jeni's innovation in high esteem, naturally admiring both competitors as they share friendly space along not-too-distant stretches of High Street.

It also carries through to the savory side of Ritzy's menu, with classics such as natural casing hot dogs, long known to "pop when you bite 'em," and a PB&J almost as famous as the ice cream, featuring fresh strawberries, crushed nuts, strawberry jelly and peanut butter on two delicious pieces of Texas toast. Build-your-own burgers are named in order of the number of patties: the Itzy Ritzy, the Ritz (a double) and the Grand Ritz (a triple), all topped as you watch to "complete your masterpiece."

While the COVID-19 pandemic slowed plans to add additional locations, the second generation is being patient and focusing first on its product and people. Ritzy's modern mid-century motif matches its menu of comfort food favorites, delivering a taste of nostalgia alongside a second chance to experience its award-winning quality. A classic comeback story, centered on being a central point for the neighborhood it serves—whether it's burgers and fries, a cup or a cone.

Inside Scoop: When People *(the Magazine) Came Calling*

Only four years after opening the original "G.D. Ritzy's Luxury Grill & Ice Creams," Graydon got a call from *People* magazine, asking if Ritzy's would like to be considered for its upcoming ranking of America's best ice creams. "Of course we were hopeful and so thankful when they called us," Graydon remembers, "at the time though we thought we'd be lost in the shuffle with the LA, NYC, San Francisco, Miami, Chicago, Boston, etc. submissions." But after sending some of Ritzy's flavors on dry ice to *People*'s taste test, Ritzy's chocolate put Columbus on the map (fourth place went to Graeter's in Cincinnati).

In the June 4 article, *People* describes the winning flavor as a blend of "Dutch cocoa with cocoa liqueurs and cocoa powders, milk, cream, eggs and sugar, but no stabilizers or emulsifiers. Butterfat is high (16 percent) and air content moderate (25 percent)." A dip back in the day set customers back between eighty-nine and ninety-nine cents (at the time, flavors were classified as either "Select" or "Elite"), and the chain's seventy-five stores drew people even in winter, as "one fanatic drives over 200 miles from Flint, Michigan to load a special freezer in his car."

HARTZLER FAMILY DAIRY

https://www.hartzlerdairy.com/

Brothers Joe and John Hartzler grew up two of eight children on a family farm in Wooster, Ohio. Their parents, Harold and Patricia, had started farming in the heart of Wayne County in the early 1950s, raising their family on and from the land. After nearly forty years of farming, Harold—or Grandpa Hartzler, as he became known—gathered the family and directed them toward the next evolution, a milk processing plant and storefront location that opened in 1996.

"Our biggest challenge when we first opened was that we were the first new dairy to open in Ohio for forty years," recalls Joe. "Government agencies didn't know how to handle us because it had been so long since the last dairy opened. They did not have an employee that knew the ins and outs of opening this new dairy enterprise."

Carrying on their father's philosophy of "as nature intended," Joe and John strive to produce minimally processed, wholesome products that taste as they should. Applying this to ice cream means that all of the milk used is locally sourced. In fact, the operation is vertically integrated to control the process from planting the seed to handing the customer the final product—literally from ground, to feed, to cow, to milk, to ice cream. Sustainable farming practices and pasture-fed cows, free from hormones, as well as low-temperature vat pasteurization, allow Hartzler milk to retain a majority of its enzymes, preserving its most natural state and aiding digestion. This also gives the milk a unique quality, which leads to a custom ice cream mix that offers a creamier mouthfeel.

A Hartzler Family Dairy seasonal pint. *Credit Hartzler Family Dairy.*

When it comes to flavors, the brothers have been inspired to experiment, pulling from family memories and stories of growing up on the farm. Joe's personal favorite recalls their mom picking wild tea leaves from a ditch behind the house and using them to make iced tea. The uniquely named Ditch Tea Delight brings him back with minty memories, featuring mint ice cream with a chocolate swirl and chocolate cookie pieces. Another flavor with an interesting moniker, Hot Mud, features chocolate ice cream with chocolate cookie pieces and marshmallow crème. Fan favorite Heifer Trails is Hartzler's take on the state's favorite combination of chocolate and peanut butter, with a peanut butter ice cream base, peanut butter swirl, peanut butter cups and chocolate chips.

The ice cream shop itself has expanded over the years, with a keen focus on customer experience. Other menu items that match the quality of the milk products are featured, such as a combination of locally grown vegetables, locally made bread and Boar's Head deli meats to create high-quality sandwiches. Pastries are baked in-house, both for sale in the shop and as ingredients for the ice cream, including brownies and vanilla wafers; chocolate chip cookies are used for ice cream sandwiches and house-made custard is used in ice cream cakes. Scones and muffins round out the offering, complementing the coffee side of the business, a mutually beneficial partnership with Heartwood Coffee Roastery that allows the dairy shop to operate as a full coffee and espresso bar, sustaining business in the colder, less ice cream friendly months. Coming full circle to the quality of the milk itself, Joe says, "We have seen that coffee shops are becoming a bigger part of our customer base as our milk creates a better quality coffee drink," adding, "Many of our milk customers are health conscious. We see the industry as a whole needing to serve a more educated and health-conscious group. We want to create new flavor combinations using fewer and more simple ingredients."

This approach carries their father's founding philosophy through to the company's sleek pint packaging (milk is still bottled in glass accordingly—also because glass is nonporous and maintains freshness better) and commitment to showcasing the high-quality dairy. "Wayne County is known as the dairy capital of Ohio," says Joe. "It's a rural community though we are in Wooster, the county seat and the largest city around. This creates a unique environment of conservative and liberal values—who all love ice cream."

For the past twenty-five years, Hartzler Family Dairy has been welcoming all of those ice cream–loving Ohioans to visit their family-oriented offering. The location was chosen for easy accessibility and designed with both indoor and outdoor seating, as well as retail offerings and two playgrounds. Whether you visit the farm directly (June brings National Dairy Month and its annual customer appreciation day with one-dollar scoops), find Hartzler at the Wayne County Fair or pick up a pint at retail alongside your gallon of Hartzler milk, you'll know you're tasting the truest expression of dairy. As the Hartzler family believes, "Nature does all the hard work here. The less you process milk, the easier it is to digest, it's that simple," which is why their products are "Made Better, Tastes Better, and Better for You."

JENI'S SPLENDID ICE CREAMS

https://jenis.com/

She's been dubbed the queen of ice cream by outlets ranging from *CherryBombe* to *Edible* and *Forbes*, but Jeni Britton Bauer praises instead the women she's dubbed the "founding mothers of ice cream," including Aunt Sallie Shadd, First Lady Dolley Madison and Nancy Johnson. Shadd, a freed slave in late-1700s Delaware, opened a catering business and became so famous for a frozen blend of cream, sugar and fruit that she's rumored to have inspired Madison to serve it at her husband's 1813 inaugural ball. Then, in 1843, Johnson took the craft one giant step further, inventing the first hand-cranked ice cream freezer.

Right: Jeni Britton Bauer, every bit the "modern mother of ice cream." *Jeni's Splendid Ice Creams*.

Below: Jeni's Splendid Ice Creams at the North Market. *Jeni's Splendid Ice Creams*.

"Trends in the ice cream industry move slowly," says Jeni. "For the first one hundred years [citing the period roughly between 1876 and 1976], it was about quality, establishing classics. Then, it became more personality driven, with brands like Ben & Jerry's [founded in 1978]. Newer shops [since around 2007] are about ice cream as an experience."

Jeni's Splendid Ice Creams, which began in Columbus in 2002, is certainly that, focused on both the flavor—defined by Jeni as "the essential character of something or someone"—as well as the feeling that ice cream facilitates, the notion that customers visiting one of the brands now fifty-plus locations in a dozen states are "here to get to know someone better."

But much like the industry itself, Jeni's empire wasn't built overnight. She took a less direct path that wound through art school, a job at a rustic bakery/pastry shop and a brief consideration of pursuing a profession as a perfumer—but it all actually started in ice cream. "I was the first employee of the Graeter's location on Lane Avenue when I was in high school," recalls Jeni, who realized the full-circle opportunity when her passions collided, allowing her to creatively express herself in the artistically sensory sweet treat.

The initial iteration of this pursuit started in Columbus's North Market in 1996 as Scream, with Jeni sourcing ingredients from the indoor public market's other purveyors, from farmers to the spice shop, cheesemakers to chocolatiers, even the wine seller and ethnic food stalls. Playing with distinct flavors and leaning heavily toward her artistic background, this first foray was a true learning experience, closing in 2000 to revamp the business plan, rebrand and reopen in 2002 as Jeni's Splendid Ice Creams. This time, Jeni focused on the craveable flavors that customers had come to love, ensuring constants stayed on the menu so they had a reason to return, while experimenting with seasonally inspired flavors in rotation. The combination both created balance for the brand and allowed loyalists to spread the word, building a following for flavors like Jeni's signature Salty Caramel and a community of fans.

A Jeni's original, Salty Caramel, in an original hand-labeled pint. *Jeni's Splendid Ice Creams.*

Symbolic of Jeni's bespoke flavors, which she says are "about emotion, nostalgia, discovery, delight," Salty Caramel is one of the brand's icons, an instant hit and enduring favorite. Inspired by her time working with French pastry chefs at La Chatelaine, another job Jeni held as a high schooler, she misheard the chef's description of the "salted" caramel from his hometown in Brittany as "salty." Interpreting this to mean even more intense and extra-salty, almost like Scandinavian licorice, Jeni used the concept as the basis to create a perfect balance of salty and sweet, still made today by fire toasting sugar for a nutty caramel, then enhancing its butteriness with grass-grazed milk and a generous pinch of sea salt. It's a combination so inspiring that one Columbus-based female band formed in 2012 even named itself the Salty Caramels after it—an equally sweet addition to the local music scene.

As for Jeni's personal favorites, she's torn between another early favorite, Brown Butter Almond Brittle—a menu mainstay since its 2009 introduction, featuring her take on beloved Scandinavian treat krokan, a toffee-like candy made with butter, almonds and caramelized sugar (author Roald Dahl was such a fan, he wrote about the taste experience from his childhood)—and a new nod to nostalgia, High Five Candy Bar, introduced in the summer of 2021, an homage to Jeni's all-time favorite combination of peanut butter, caramel, chocolate and pretzels in "perfect harmony," with a secret (or not so) ingredient, honey, which adds a nougat-like flavor and texture. Part of that summer's Ice Cream Truck collection and made specifically for distribution at Whole Foods, the flavor rivals another Jeni's icon, Salted Peanut Butter with Chocolate Flecks (originally called the Buckeye State).

The list of fan favorite flavors turned brand bastions goes on in both signatures, such as Brambleberry Crisp and the brand's equally loved chocolates—Milkiest, made with condensed milk, and Darkest, achieved by using three times more chocolate than Jeni was taught at ice cream school (yes, ice cream school)—and seasonals, like summer's aptly named Golden Nectar, fall's favorite Pumpkin Roll and winter's new Maple Soaked Pancake.

Maintaining her role in creating and naming most of the brand's flavors, while welcoming contributions from everyone at the company, Jeni says her flavors are a "reflection of the moment we are all in at any given time." The brand worked hard

A signature and founder favorite: the modern classic Brown Butter Almond Brittle. *Jeni's Splendid Ice Creams.*

to expand its offering without sacrificing its signature taste and texture when it launched dairy-free flavors in 2019, with the first four including Cold Brew with Coconut Cream, Dark Chocolate Truffle, Texas Sheet Cake and Roasted Peanut Butter and Strawberry Jam. "We spent a decade developing dairy free," says Jeni, with the goal of balancing out some of the effects of dairy production on the planet and leveraging botanical creams and fats to achieve a similarly beautiful mouthfeel to the original lineup. "It's not about eliminating but rather cutting back," she adds, noting that the shop's signature Trio offering (three half scoops) lends itself well to pairing dairy and dairy-free options for those who don't have dietary restrictions.

If not a queen, Jeni is certainly an industry pioneer equal to the founding mothers of ice cream, having started the spread of artisanal ice cream from the middle of America not only around the country but across the world. She credits both her own and the company's Ohio roots, noting that Ohio was the first state that wasn't a colony of the British empire and one that birthed eight presidents; its cities were founded around farming, education and, most of all, community. Jeni's definition of character, which she attributes to being made up of person and place, has always been a driving factor, as she "built the company as if [she was] twelve and just thought that's how it should be." With B Corp status, indicating the "highest standards of verified social and environmental performance, public transparency, and legal accountability to balance profit and purpose," Jeni's is committed to the belief that "business can be a powerful force for good." Direct and fair trade relationships with suppliers and a fellowship model of growers and producers include Ohio dairy farms Smith's in Orrville and Arps in Defiance, as well as Hirsch Fruit Farm in Chillicothe, Mackenzie Creamery in Hiram and Columbus's own Middle West Spirits.

As for future pursuits, Jeni is always asking, "What can ice cream be now?" Believing that we've yet to see the golden age of ice cream, she says changes industrywide are "just beginning, with better technology, transportation and communication." Furthermore, she sees service as "especially important in ice cream as it's always a special moment." Special indeed, whether you're at one of Jeni's scoop shops celebrating National Ice Cream for Breakfast Day (the first Saturday in February), the first day of summer or just a typical Tuesday, as every day at Jeni's is simply splendid.

Strawberry fields forever: going straight to the source at Hirsch Fruit Farm. *Jeni's Splendid Ice Creams*.

A modern view of North Market, where it all began for Jeni's Splendid Ice Creams. *Jeni's Splendid Ice Creams.*

SCOOPING UP JENI'S AT HOME

Jeni's can be found in Scoop Shops and at grocers nationwide and also offers direct-to-consumer shipping of everything from pints to party boxes called "Collections," ranging from Happy Birthday to Newborn Baby and from Top Sellers to Jeni's Picks, Thank You, Gluten-Free and Street Treats—Jeni's take on those grab-and-go cups with the spoon tucked right under the lid—available in an assortment of fun flavors.

To start following in Jeni's footsteps, grab a copy of her *New York Times* best-selling and 2012 James Beard Award–winning cookbook, *Jeni's Splendid Ice Creams at Home*, which the *Wall Street Journal* called the "homemade–ice cream–making Bible"; its 2014 follow-up, *Jeni's Splendid Ice Cream Desserts*; or 2019's *The Artisanal Kitchen: Perfect Homemade Ice Cream*, part of a series spotlighting chefs at the top of their respective crafts. (Spoiler alert: to achieve the rich mouthfeel of Jeni's at home, she employs a cream cheese hack in the book's recipes, though the simmering process is exactly as they do it for the shop's version.)

Inside Scoop: Torn on Your Trio?

Upgrade to a Flight, ten half-scoops of Jeni's most popular flavors served in a dish, featuring Brown Butter Almond Brittle, Gooey Butter Cake, Darkest Chocolate, Coffee with Cream and Sugar, Brambleberry Crisp, Salty Caramel Salted Peanut Butter with Chocolate Flecks, Honey Vanilla Bean, Wildberry Lavender and Rainbow Buttermilk Frozen Yogurt.

MASON'S CREAMERY

https://www.masonscreamery.com/

One year, for Helen Qin's birthday, her then-boyfriend Jesse Mason bought her an ice cream maker. She smiled and thanked him, of course; the gesture was sweet and based on her insatiable love for the product—but, she then told him, she didn't actually want to make her own ice cream. So he did, taking the present and turning it into an actual gift, making her experimental fun flavors, which she immediately loved the texture of, saying, "It just tastes different when it's right out of the batch."

The pair, who met in Los Angeles and had long been fans of shops like Sweet Rose Creamery—often waiting an hour in line at the Santa Monica shop, hungry from a hike in Brentwood—relocated to Jesse's hometown of Cleveland in 2013. Happily, they found a thriving food scene not unlike the one they'd experienced while living in Oakland, California, and an energetic city with lots of events that embraced artisanal, small-batch businesses.

Jumping right in, Jesse leveraged previous experience in the service industry alongside his graphic design background to build out a mobile cart. Renting space at the Cleveland Culinary Launch and Kitchen, the couple geared up for the spring season, applying to farmers markets and events such as the Cleveland Asian Festival. Born in China, Helen tapped into her heritage for flavor inspiration, using ube, a purple yam often found in Filipino desserts, for a nuttier take on vanilla—with instantly Instagrammable color. That first foray into the Cleveland Asian Festival, with its two thousand attendees, was a fast introduction to the food scene.

After a summer spent working events five days a week and making ice cream the other two, Mason's had cultivated such a following that residents of Ohio City reached out, letting Jesse and Helen know that Ohio City Ice Cream (formerly Dairy Delight) was closing that August after operating since

Not-so-simple soft serve topped with French Toast Crunch cereal (see if you can spot the ramen bowl in the Mason's logo behind). *Jesse Mason.*

the 1960s. Loving the neighborhood (the couple lives there as well) and hidden-gem location, they stepped up to the challenge of renovating the once-walk-up-only, closed-in-winter space to accommodate seating and stay open year-round. But colder temps still bring change to the space, as Mason's transforms into a ramen shop from late fall (November) through early spring (March/April).

"Coming from LA, it was hard to find tonkatsu ramen at the time in Cleveland," recalls Helen, "so once again, Jesse decided to make his own and introduce people to it. When we quickly sold out of our first batch (thirty servings), we decided to do a monthly pop-up to keep business going in the winter months. We were selling out of three hundred bowls in about an hour and a half each day so, a few years ago, we decided to focus on ramen solely in the winter."

A super fun and unexpected twist in the story, for sure, but let's get back to the ice cream. From that original ube to a rotating weekly flavor offering of vegan soft serve, Mason's focuses on small batches using the best possible ingredients, working with local farms like Quarry Hill when possible. "Our flavors come from traveling and trying different foods from different countries," says Helen. "The base idea is a love of food and how it can bring people together from different cultures." Alongside these unique flavors are twists on classics, such as cereal-based creations using Captain Crunch, Fruity Pebbles and Lucky Charms. Accommodating various dietary restrictions also ensures there's an offering for everyone, and all recipes are egg free.

Founder favorite flavors include Jesse's nectarine sorbet (which has origins in Sweet Rose Creamery) and Helen's summer staple, strawberry made with real, fresh strawberries. Any of these stunning options stands out even more in an egg waffle, Hong Kong's answer to the waffle cone, made on a special machine to achieve the bubble/pancake-like look and taste. Other house-made specials include a banana split that features banana bread as its base, as well as churros and cookies for ice cream sandwiches. Even the whipped cream is made in-house, and it goes beyond the basic, with options like marzipan and peanut butter whip. Shakes, floats and even ice cream–topped teas round out the menu, with inspired seasonal variations bringing fun to holidays like Halloween and St. Patrick's Day.

Calzone ice cream in a homemade waffle cone. *Jesse Mason.*

After seven summers in Ohio City, Mason's has become a cornerstone of the community, drawing crowds to its lawn on warm nights and hosting events with neighborhood partners and charitable organizations. One such gathering, dubbed Pie Day, was brought together over a Twitter debate on crumble crust versus traditional pie topping. Hosting the inaugural event in August 2021, Mason's partnered with Cleveland radio figure Jimmy Malone and his college scholarship program to raise over $8,000 and hopes to make it an annual event.

Maintaining this sense of community and continuity is important to both Helen and Jesse throughout the year. Bringing people together to try new things, whether it's winter's ramen or summer's scoops and soft serves, Mason's invites the neighborhood to make it their meeting place. In fact, the sentiment is quite literally written right on the exterior wall, brightly exclaiming, "Come Over All The Time!"

CRMD

https://www.getcrmd.com/

One night in 2018, Benjamin Stoyka and Kristina "Tina" Duong decided to take a road trip. The pair had just been handed a $300,000 estimate for renovations to a space they were planning to rent in their hometown of Cleveland, their aspirations of opening a fresh take on a mom-and-pop ice cream shop nearly dashed.

Having stumbled across a listing on High Street in Columbus, positioned perfectly in the bustling Short North, they drove down early that next October morning to check out the area and the space itself, a former art gallery that had been vacant for years. Almost instantly, visions of sugar filled

CRMD on High Street in the Short North. *CRMD.*

their heads and the perfectly sized space, though they knew literally nothing about building a restaurant. By January 2019, when they took ownership, they had both a business plan and a contractor to help with design, but they did much of the work themselves to keep costs down. They worked through both the winter and spring, and CRMD finally opened its doors for the first time on July 19, 2019, a simple, sleek, black-and-white space with a focus on bold pops of color from sixteen unique flavors and the signature, highly Instagrammable puffle cone.

First, let's talk flavors. Starting with high-quality ingredients and drawing inspiration from experiences the couple had traveling the world, as well as nods to their Ohio roots and new hometown, the backstories bring even more depth to each flavor. Ben and Tina's personal favorite is a testament to the impact of memory on taste, as well as their go-to for an energy boost on a long workday at the shop. "We sampled about 20 coffees in Vietnam and found the one we liked the best to import for our 'Viet Coffee' flavor," says Ben. "I think the story and experiences from that trip really stood out as well and it seems like it was just yesterday." Closer to home, a nod to the city that almost got them started, the CLE Brownie Bites, is a subtle nudge to their roots, featuring brownie bites in vanilla ice cream, tinted orange for the Cleveland Browns football team. And the eye-catching variations on vanilla don't stop there, with Black Vanilla shaded, as its name implies, with the addition of coconut-activated charcoal (the flavor is also paired with lemon in a swirl named for the Columbus soccer team's fan base, the Nordecke Crew); Nilla Cookie Dough, featuring pieces of cookie dough in a bright shade of blue; and Cookies and CRMD, which spins the color wheel to purple for a not-so-classic cookies and cream. Options for those with dietary preferences or restrictions round out the menu with vegetarian/vegan, gluten- and dairy-free ice creams and sorbets made equally as colorful as their dairy-based counterparts.

And then there's that cone. Ben and Tina first came across the puffle cone, also known as an egg waffle, while traveling in China. Made from an eggy, leavened batter cooked between two plates of semispherical cells, the texture is spongy; overseas, they're eaten more like Americans would French fries. Then, in Vietnam, the couple found a related street food, tiny bite-sized waffle cakes. They took the basics of both recipes and added their own touch, and the resulting combination is a signature style that pairs perfectly with—and serves as a photo-ready backdrop for—your favorite flavor.

With a location central to the city of Columbus, situated directly between downtown and the campus of the Ohio State University, CRMD's fun approach attracts a wide variety of fans, from families to college kids and young professionals to groups of grandparents. "We see a very wide range of culture," says Ben, adding that "Columbus is a melting pot, the schools and big corporate offices bring people from all over and when you look around you can see it. There are restaurants that have any type of food you can desire and that's caused by the years and years of cultural diversity being built up in the city. That's one of the things we love about Columbus."

Partnerships with some of those restaurants and other local purveyors, such as bakeries and breweries, have helped expand awareness and establish

Vegan Vanilla Nut Swirl, made using CRMD's coconut cream vegan ice cream mix, adding coconut-activated charcoal to their peanut butter mix to make the peanut butter black and swirling them together for a marbling effect. *Dakota Dean, @dakotadeanvisualmedia.*

roots in Columbus. Future plans for CRMD include potential expansion to big cities, possibly near college campuses, areas that tend to be open to something different and where people seek out opportunities to try new things. They feel they're in good company, following in the footsteps of the likes of Graeter's and Jeni's, as well as other ice cream companies founded in Ohio that have had success expanding. And if Cleveland plays its cards right this time, it just might get its CRMD location someday, too.

THE OHIO ICE CREAM TRAIL

Find All of the Adventurous Ohio Trails at https://trails.ohio.org/

Since 2015, when TourismOhio launched the "Find It Here" slogan as an umbrella for the diverse array of activities the state has to offer both residents and visitors, it introduced a complementary group of trails, of which there are presently nearly seventy to choose from. Spanning a wide variety of interests and attractions, there are trails for historical figures and happenings (the Hopalong Cassidy Trail and the Clermont County Freedom Trail); hobbies, such as birding and quilt making, aviation and art; and even a haunted trail. And just when all of that exploring leaves one hungry, there are trails for foodies; beer, wine and coffee drinkers; and, of course, lovers of sweet treats like doughnuts, candy and, you guessed it, ice cream.

The Ohio Ice Cream Trail was introduced in 2018 to showcase the state's rich heritage and spotlight businesses throughout the region. While TourismOhio selected the first fifteen stops, the next five were chosen by reader survey (the trail was revised in 2021 but still includes twenty stops), and a social media campaign featuring the hashtag #MyOhioScoop was introduced for visitors to share their stops.

In addition to the many stops profiled in this book, the Ohio Ice Cream Trail also features the following regional favorites.

Northeast Ohio

TOFT'S (SANDUSKY): Ohio's oldest dairy (in operation since 1900), Toft's goes direct to the source, its own farms, to make creations as fun to order as they are to eat, including Lake Erie Cookie Island Monster, Muddy's Sea Salt Slam (an homage to local Triple A baseball team the Toledo Mud Hens) and Cedar Point Cotton Candy, named for the amusement park, which also serves up its scoops. *https://toftdairy.com/*

MITCHELL'S HOMEMADE ICE CREAM (CLEVELAND): With ten locations in the greater Cleveland area, you can't miss Mitchell's. But at its flagship Ohio City shop, you can also get a glimpse behind the scenes while touring its production kitchen, learning about how it transformed a former theater into an ice cream factory and shop—and, of course, tasting as you go. Guests also learn about the brand's focus on sustainability through its environmental emphasis, local sourcing and social support. Whether you top off your tour with fan favorite flavors Blue Cosmo or Turtle Brownie, Peanut Butter Chocolate Pretzel Frozen Yogurt or the Vegan Salted Caramel Pecan, both your sweet tooth and your conscience will be more than satisfied. *https://mitchellshomemade.com/*

HONEY HUT ICE CREAM (CLEVELAND): Since 1974, when firefighter Frank Page and his family turned an old shoe repair store in their "Old Brooklyn" neighborhood into the first of what would become five Honey Hut Ice Cream stores, the neighborhood institution has been delighting customers with bespoke twists on classic flavors. Firehouse taste tests led to favorites like the signature Honey Pecan, a honey-sweetened take on butter pecan, and Orange Blossom, a riff on a Creamsicle featuring orange zest and orange blossom honey. How sweet it is! *https://gohoneyhut.com/*

ROSATI'S (NORTHFIELD CENTER): Spinning her knowledge of ice cream off into a second booming ice cream business, Marcia Page and her husband, Jim Rosati, opened Rosati's Frozen Custard in 2000 (the couple also owns the Honey Hut locations in Brecksville and Brunswick). The denser treat—featuring an egg base with less air integrated—is made in small batches hourly throughout the day, with more than 150 special flavors of custard, 1 offered each day during the April to October season, alongside classic vanilla and chocolate. Especially of note is Rosati's take on the long-lost Higbee's chocolate malt, a feature of the iconic downtown department store from the 1930s through the 1970s. *https://rosatisfrozencustard.com/*

MILK & HONEY (CANTON): This sweet shoppe is a treasured time warp for locals who love the old-school diner fare as much as the ice cream sodas and sundaes. The shop's recipe for its homemade chocolates is over fifty years old and shares the spotlight with fan favorite ice cream flavors, such as Orange Pineapple and Lake Erie Salt Mine. It's been a Canton go-to since 1962, and you can't go wrong with a sandwich and a sundae at Milk & Honey. *https://www.milkandhoneyshoppes.com/*

Northwest Ohio

THE CREAMERY (DELPHOS): Receiving the most write-in votes during the trail's launch campaign, the Creamery was an easy addition. Located in the heart of downtown Delphos, the seasonal stalwart has been lining up locals since 1982 both in its walk-up and drive-thru. Since it boasts a list of flavors "a country mile long," the decision between soft serve, hard dip, shake, sundae or malt may be a challenge, but at least it's a delicious one. *https://thecreameryofohio.com/*

The Creamery in Delphos. *The Creamery.*

LAKE CITY CREAMERY (CELINA): Known for inventive flavors—including Bananas Foster, Cinnamon Oatmeal Raisin Cookie and local loyalist obsession Pear Riesling Sorbet—Lake City Creamery doesn't disappoint when it comes to decadence. Seasonal features include Jack-O-Lantern, a pumpkin ice cream with pieces of homemade fudge and ripples of caramel, and Sweet Potato Casserole, featuring candied pecans and ripples of mallo crème. *http://www.lakecity-creamery.com/*

There are hundreds of great ice cream places across Ohio. TourismOhio's Ice Cream Trail highlights local, family-owned and nationally recognized ice cream shops across the state. Shops as numbered: (1) Toft's, (2) Sweet Moses Soda Fountain (closed), (3) Mason's Creamery, (4) Mitchell's Homemade Ice Cream, (5) Honey Hut Ice Cream, (6) Rosati's Frozen Custard, (7) Dietsch Brothers, (8) Hartzler Family Dairy, (9) Milk & Honey, (10) Handel's Homemade Ice Cream, (11) The Creamery, (12) Lake City Creamery, (13) Velvet Ice Cream, (14) Jeni's Splendid Ice Creams, (15) Johnson's Real Ice Cream, (16) Tom's Ice Cream Bowl, (17) Young's Jersey Dairy, (18) Whit's Frozen Custard (Athens location), (19) Aglamesis Brothers, (20) Graeter's. *Map by Caroline Rodrigues.*

Chapter 4

LOCAL LEGENDS

*I*f ice cream has the ability to bring people together, the small-town mom-and-pop shops that serve their communities are among the most hospitable hubs of happiness. While the businesses may have changed owners over the years, the new owners are committed to retaining the original charm, serving as shepherds for the community's central gathering spot.

Alongside ice cream, they might offer regional specialties, such as pulled chicken sandwiches in central Ohio, root beer floats in southeastern Ohio or an amped-up version of the classic hot dog, with a bespoke chili sauce that makes it a true coney.

Roadside stops, such as Zip Dip and Whipty-Do line up both the locals and tourists just passing through town for nostalgic tastes of childhood. Likewise, the Dairy Hut and King Kone invite generations to pass down memories through a shared scoop. Reviving a long-defunct predecessor, Pete's Ice Cream quickly made up for lost time and developed a fiercely loyal following, which gave it top ranks in regional voting.

Many of these operations are seasonal only, bookending each summer with their spring openings and fall closings. Both events are big affairs, the former a sure signal of warmer weather's sweet arrival and the latter causing folks to stockpile favorites to last them the long winter.

Over the decades, Ohio's deep dairy roots have helped develop an ice cream industry that, while in some ways has gone through dramatic changes, also maintains classics like these hot spots serving up the same cool treats. Embracing the past allows these hometown stalwarts to continue to thrive long into the future.

Zip Dip

https://zip-dip.com/

Many things have changed on the West Side of Cincinnati since 1950, but Zip Dip simply isn't one of them. Zip Dip is simple in its roadside stand setup, yet striking, with red and green neon lighting up the thunderbolt through its soft serve ice cream cone logo, and its seventy-year-old legacy has lived on for four generations of Cincinattians.

The stand was originally built by Charlie Metzner, who lived across the street but never operated the business, instead leasing it to two local high school teachers. Ownership changed hands twice more before Chris Torbeck purchased the business in 1987. At the helm for the past thirty-four seasons, Torbeck carries on the annual tradition of opening up the stand in March and closing it again in October, in between serving up the same flavors customers have grown up on and now bring back their kids and their kids' kids to enjoy.

Of the vanilla, chocolate, orange sorbet and swirls combining the two latter with the former, respectively, Torbeck is modest, noting that "it's standard soft serve" and that "what sets us apart is the nostalgia—everything about our building is original." But that sense of midwestern modesty is belied by brightly hued "Dip Top" flavors, including chocolate, cherry and blueberry, as well as jimmies (also known as sprinkles) ranging from rainbow to chocolate, blue to Krunch Kote. And the menu doesn't simply

Nightfall over Zip Dip. *Zip Dip.*

stop with cones but features a wide variety of sundaes (hot fudge, caramel, strawberry, peanut butter, marshmallow, mint, butterscotch, chocolate syrup, raspberry, cherry, pineapple, peach, blueberry), flurries (either fruit-based — strawberry, raspberry, cherry, pineapple, peach, blueberry—or with candy mixed in: bestselling Reese's Cup, Snickers, Butterfinger, Oreo, M&M's, Peanut M&M's, Nestlé Crunch, cookie dough, brownie bites, chocolate chips, Kit Kat, Reese's Pieces, chocolate granola, original granola, vanilla berry granola) and shakes and malts (chocolate, vanilla, Oreo, hot fudge, caramel, strawberry, peanut butter, marshmallow, mint, butterscotch, cherry, raspberry, pineapple, peach, blueberry, nectar). Phew, and that's not even mentioning the ice cream sandwiches, banana splits and slush puppies!

It's tough to pick from all those options; Chris says he's "a malt guy" and opts for the Hot Fudge Malt as his favorite treat, enjoying the creaminess of the fudge. He's also a strong-willed guy, having lobbied the local jurisdiction for the ability to install outdoor swings and picnic tables adjacent to the property. He recalls a local commissioner saying, "There is common law, and then there is common sense law." Luckily for the summer crowds, Chris prevailed.

Beyond building simple memories of summer, Zip Dip's classic charm lends itself well as the backdrop for a lifetime of milestones. Its sign plays host to annual prom invites, some of which have led to lifelong commitments. Each season sees at least a marriage proposal or two, and Zip Dip has even hosted wedding anniversary parties for couples who had their first date there decades ago. Families built on soft serve return together, with three or even four generations at the window placing their order. And never more apparent is this love for the location and one another than when a family gathers after a funeral service for a grandparent who brought them there growing up, toasting the deceased with their favorite flavor.

Taking pride in keeping tradition alive, Torbeck—who originally played down the premium nature of the product, calling it "standard soft serve"— acquiesces that "Ohio is special to the ice cream industry because, in my opinion, we are home to the best hard dip ice cream produced." He admires nearby third-generation family-owned business Graeter's, adding, "I like to compare our products by saying Zip Dip is the Graeter's of soft serve." He also admires other family-run soft serve shops, including Putz's Creamy Whip, the first in the city.

The future of Zip Dip promises to maintain the past, keeping the 1950s look and decor as well as sticking to its menu staples. Old-fashioned delights and a nowadays novel design are sure to make this vintage roadside stand a modern marvel for many years to come.

What the What Is Creamy Whip?
And Putz's, a Local Icon

https://www.putzscreamywhip.com/

A term for both place and product, creamy whip—the regional term for soft serve common in Cincinnati (especially on the West Side of town)—likely came into use during the mid-1950s and early 1960s. It was then that Putz's, which had started as a scoop ice cream business in 1938, transitioned under second-generation owners Gertie and Ray Ehrhardt, who brought in two new Electro-Freeze ice cream machines to make their now-famous creamy whip.

The term became so synonymous with the product that locals associate "soft serve" with a completely different thing, a commoditized version mass-produced at fast-food restaurants rather than lovingly crafted at the mom-and-pop shops dotting the area's landscape. One loyalist, Bob Woodiwiss, an accomplished advertising copywriter who grew up in the area, delves deep in a 2011 piece for *Cincinnati Magazine*, "Creamy Whip & Other Delights," breaking down the distinction between the soft serve that's been commoditized by fast-food restaurants and the creamy whip he grew up with and still pursues with vigorous delight each season. In fact, according to Bob, seasonality is another bespoke element of the classic creamy whip spot, as limited availability adds to the charm, requiring visits as frequent as the summer is fleeting.

Cincinnati's *CityBeat* agrees with Bob about another requirement: to be classified as a creamy whip, an operation should maintain smaller-scale and somewhat humble surroundings. In fact, the publication's 2020 roundup of "17 Essential Cincinnati Creamy Whips You Need to Visit This Summer" noted that "real creamy whip must come from a creamy whip (Orange Leaf is not a creamy whip), which generally looks like a shack with a walk-up window and line of little leaguers waiting to order up something sweet after a ballgame." Proper aesthetics established, Bob further defines the subcategory as both "healthier," based on its lower butterfat content (4 to 6 percent in creamy whip versus 10 to 16 percent in traditional ice cream) and greater value, in that most have maintained prices accessible with a young child's allowance (something that Bob argues isn't always the case at more "boutique"-type ice cream establishments).

Whether it all started at Putz's (an old menu board referred to the product as "Creamy Whip Cones," even when the business's name was "Putz's Dairy Freeze"; the current location, opened in the mid-1950s, bears the name "Putz's Creamy Whip" proudly across the front), this creamy whip certainly has stood the test of time, becoming the standard-bearer for many purists. The same two machines purchased in 1954 and 1955 remain in full-time operation today, with the fourth and fifth generations now shepherding the business each season, giving credit to those two machines for distinguishing their product from other creamy whips in town.

But Putz's legacy goes beyond the cone and into the community. In 1971, third-generation owner Ray "Lil" Ehrhardt successfully petitioned President Richard Nixon to rework plans for the I-74 expressway, ensuring the road would be built far enough back to maintain operations. Then, in 1987, Putz's was honored for its significance when the city council unanimously voted to rename the section of Baltimore Avenue on which it sits "Putz's Place."

Putz's, home of the creamy whip. *Putz's Creamy Whip.*

Eternalizing it even further, the Colerain Boosters and playwright Dick Ruehrwein wrote and performed a play after the shop, twice putting on *Putz's Creamy Whip* as a stage production.

Putz's was founded by a family and built on the shared memories of families. Stories abound of couples that met in line at Putz's or got engaged across one of Putz's picnic tables, themes duplicated at many similar shops in town. One couple, as crazy for creamy whip as they were for one another, even asked Grandpa Putz if they could marry on the roof of the shop. When asked about retirement, Grandma Gertie laughed, saying that by then, she and her husband, Ray, had "ice cream in our veins instead of blood."

Fourth-generation owners Donna and Jack Borgman recall the term *creamy whip* being reserved for members of the I Buy Good Association, started in the mid-1970s by Bob Hook and Jim Flint, of which Gertie and Ray were members. Membership not only offered the perks of discounts from about ten suppliers but, most importantly, also gave a shop the right to call itself a creamy whip. In fact, Donna recalls someone using the name without belonging to the association and being forced to change it. Jack believes there were members in nearby northern Kentucky and just across the border in Indiana, though the total number of shops is unknown.

Though the association ceased operations in about 2000, after the passing of both Bob and Jim, the term endures, just like Putz's itself, which, in 2020, was passed down to Donna and Jim's son, Raymond, and daughter-in-law, Mindi. After learning the business inside and out since her first job there at age fifteen, stepping up to the challenge of eighty-plus-hour weeks in Putz's high season was a no brainer for Mindi; after all, it's the only place she's ever worked. Her focus is singular: continuing the family legacy for a fifth generation, thereby ensuring the coveted term *creamy whip* endures.

Whether it's Putz's, Granny's (a now-shuttered shop with an equally memorable founder Bob fondly recalls from frequent visits in the '90s) or Whipty-Do (a slightly more modern take—if only because it offers Flavor Burst, a technology that adorns twists with a syrup stripe—located in eastern suburb of Maineville), Bob and his fellow Cincinnattians continue their long love affair with creamy whip: the product, the places and the people that make it not simply soft serve.

WHIPTY-DO

https://www.whipty-do.com

When Kristen Fields and her husband, Joe, opened Whipty-Do in 2009, it may have been the couple's first small business, but it wasn't the first time Kristen had been involved with the space: it was formerly the site of her father's optometry practice in the mid-1990s. Kristen recalls a childhood spent with the "all hands on deck" mentality needed to own and operate a family business. Her father's own success caused him to move to a larger building after a number of years, and when the space became available, Kristen and Joe jumped at the opportunity to build their own business with this connection.

Knowing they wanted to open a business, Kristen and Joe chose ice cream because it's a happy business, a business of bringing joy to others. "There is nothing like seeing the face of a child—or even an adult—light up when you hand them their cone, or cheering someone up who has had a bad day, or even helping to celebrate with our guests." She adds, "Ice cream is pure and simple, a joy for others, and I am so happy to be able to deliver this to my guests every single day."

Her enthusiasm is simply infectious and has helped build a following, bringing loyal customers from as far as Indiana, Illinois and Kentucky. "A guest came to visit from Illinois and was raving about our ice cream, telling me that she only wants to come home when we are open," says Kristen, happy to hear the shared passion and appreciation for the shop's commitment to quality. She adds, "We like to be creative and try new things, while still always offering the classics."

Folks travel for miles for the creamy quality of Whipty-Do's classic soft serve. *Whipty-Do.*

One such classic, which quickly put Whipty-Do on the creamy whip map in greater Cincinnati, is the best-selling blueberry ice cream. Whipty-Do is located just ten minutes from Kings Island Amusement Park, and the opportunity to eat the same ice cream that has long been a popular park treat brings people to Whipty-Do from all over the city. It's one of only a few shops that offers this niche—but locally well loved—product, with the distinctive option to customize it with any combination of flavors and toppings one desires, and this colorful menu staple is central to Whipty-Do's offering. Another hometown favorite, Grippo's potato chips, which have a spicy barbecue flavor, are rolled around creamy soft serve for a polarizing promotion that Kristen absolutely loves.

Monthly specials—such as mint-flavored ice cream and Lucky Charms cereal for St. Patrick's Day, pretzels in April and Nutter Butter cookies in September—keep things fresh, but it's June that proves most popular. Transformed into Junutella, homemade waffle cones are lined with namesake Nutella and paired with Strawberry or Raspberry Dole Whip for the most special of specialty months.

Kristen herself keeps it classic with either a twist cone covered in sprinkles or a vanilla dipped in chocolate, following in the footsteps of her father for her first order of the season. Joe channels childhood memories for his go-to milkshake, the peanut butter, which also inspired him to create "Secret Menu" top seller the Peanut Butter Beast (it's so proprietary that, while the rest of the undercover options are accessible on Whipty-Do's website, details about the Beast are available only by asking). From the Next Level (an Oreo malt with a pump of vanilla) to the Unicorn McSprinkle Twinkle (blue goo flavor burst, marshmallow, rainbow sprinkles), offerings from shakes to sodas, floats to icebergs (ice cream floating in a sea of slushie) and sundaes to signature Whipty-Whirls are as fun to order as they are to eat.

Fun is key at Whipty-Do, with the experience as important as the product. After nine years as a walk-up only, a drive-thru was added in 2018, allowing the season to extend longer. While the regular season runs from mid-February through late October/early November, weekend-long pop-ups bring the crowds back for a temporary taste around key holidays. These "Winter Weekends"—when Whipty-Do is decorated in Christmas lights, with music blasting and specialty limited-time-only menu items like Frozen Hot Chocolate and Peppermint soft serve, plus extra treats and giveaways—are highly anticipated both for the guests and staff.

Twelve years ago, as twenty-somethings, Kristen and Joe took a business idea, a passion and a risk (opening a restaurant is always one, but to do

Proposing "I do" at Whipty-Do. *Whipty-Do.*

it during a national recession amplifies the uncertainty) and met the challenge with commitment to the community, dedication to the offering and the resilience she'd seen during her own childhood spent building her father's business. She hopes that their children, who now spend many hours at Whipty-Do alongside them, see their parents' success in a similar and perhaps tastier light.

THE DAIRY HUT

https://www.dairy-hut.com/

Since 1973, summer in Pataskala has meant one thing: standing in line at the Dairy Hut. A roadside institution now in its third ownership, the ten-foot-by-twenty-foot building (which was relocated to its current spot after a previous life selling apples) holds not only superb soft serve and a super-secretive coney sauce but also season after season of simple yet significant memories.

The Dairy Hut, late 1970s. *The Dairy Hut.*

The Dairy Hut: a long legacy of hosting Little Leaguers. *The Dairy Hut.*

Current owners Jeff and Caitlyn Heimerl took ownership from the long-standing second-generation Bocock family in 2021, after Gary Bocock; his wife, Karen; and their children Stacy and Shane (with his wife, Cherish, and daughter Ashley) ran the operation for forty-two years. In 1979, Bocock and his father, Calvin, originally door-to-door milkmen, purchased the Dairy Hut, originally founded in 1973, from their customers Glenn and Rod McIntosh and Rod's brother-in-law Dale Foor. For twenty-seven years, Calvin and Gary, along with a single employee at the beginning, built up the business, including over twenty-four ice cream flavors—and that coney sauce recipe, which is locked in a vault and known to only three people.

Serving the community of Pataskala from April through September each year, the Bococks saw generations of families grow up in the small town, each returning with the next generation. Among them were Jeff and Caitlyn, who began dating in high school and purchased their first house in Pataskala in 2012. "We started our life together going to the Dairy Hut," recalls Caitlyn, now a mom of three, "and we continued to take our kids there. It's been a staple in our life and relationship." The young farming family from Johnstown set their sights on being a part of the shop's legacy when, five years before taking over the business, Jeff began calling Gary each summer to let him know that if they ever wanted to sell, Jeff and Caitlyn would be interested in buying it. Their passion and ties to the community paid off, with Gary and Karen helping to create a seamless transition in a difficult time, during the ongoing COVID-19 pandemic, which had brought about the creation of the "world's longest drive-thru" during the 2020 season.

The Heimerls and their three children, Shiloh (five), Maesyn (three) and Baylor (who was born April 23, 2021, and has lived under the counter since he was four days old), wanted everyone to know that the Dairy Hut is still the Dairy Hut, so while they've made cosmetic updates and added a few new items, the core menu remains. Fun additions driven by their young girls include birthday cake as an ice cream flavor and a new Unicorn Sundae. Seasonal items, such as a Peach Blitzer and Peach Sundae, run during peak peach season, followed by apple and pumpkin variations. But the number one item sold out of the Dairy Hut window is the Buckeye Sundae, a triple-layer stunner that starts with vanilla soft serve topped with hot fudge, then more vanilla soft serve topped with peanut butter sauce, then more vanilla soft serve topped with whipped cream and finished with a flourish of Reese's peanut butter cups.

Ribbon cutting for the newest owners of the Dairy Hut. *The Dairy Hut.*

The Dairy Hut, an extended family. *The Dairy Hut.*

Caitlyn loves the creative side of the business, as well as the tradition of staffers getting their friends jobs, with many siblings following in their parents' footsteps of working there. A close-knit group is a good thing in the small space, which can have up to seven staffers working on a busy night. With two soft serve machines, it's a well-choreographed dance to build each order, starting with the right barrel for either vanilla, chocolate, twist or milkshake mix and adding flavors and toppings. But speed is still of the essence when it comes to cold ice cream on a hot summer night, which is why the drive-thru order time is a mere five and a half minutes (walk-ups are now also welcome again).

After working "undercover" at the end of the 2020 season to get a feel for the business and ensure it was the right fit, Caitlyn says that while "farming is hard work both mentally and physically, this is even harder, but so rewarding." She loves the family atmosphere among the staff and wants it to be their second home; she's looking forward to them bringing their children back when her own are working there someday.

With a redesigned interior and menu board for the 2021 season, the Heimerls hit the ground running, and they have plans to consolidate the storage facility and rework the outdoor space for 2022. But beyond operational improvements, the Dairy Hut will maintain its legacy in the small-town community so that future generations can experience the old-fashioned family values built by generations past and carried on today.

Inside Scoop: More on That Coney Sauce

On the hot side of the menu, that coney sauce goes on its namesake hot dog in both regular six-inch and footlong options, as well as atop tortilla chips alongside nacho cheese in the Nachos Supreme. At the end of the season, customers stock up on pints to get them through the off season, even standing in the rain in what Gary recalls as "a parade of colorful umbrellas."

KING KONE

https://www.king-kone.com/

Though it's changed names throughout its seventy-plus-year history, the local Chardon ice cream stop has remained an iconic sign of summer to its community. Current owner Gail Hewitt grew up in the neighborhood and recalls her cousin working there when they were teenagers and it was called Country Custard. When Hewitt and her husband, Mitch, along with their four children, bought the business ten years ago, they became a part of the long legacy, carrying it forward in its current iteration, King Kone.

Bright pink and mint green make it hard to miss driving down Grant Street or Route 6 through the small town in northeast Ohio, and the namesake mascot stands out equally, a very royal scoop of mint chocolate chip on a classic cake cone, crowned with a king's jewels and licking a lip. His counterpart, an equally adorable queen of a sprinkle cone, nods to the soft serve side of the business on both the building and its matching mobile ice cream truck.

King Kone has an expansive menu of both hard and soft serve flavors, along with shakes, sundaes, slushies, flurries and floats. Over thirty flavors of hard serve come from Hershey's, while the thick and creamy soft serve is made in-house with a twenty-four-flavor machine. The Hewitts brought fun menu changes, including unique creations of toppings and sauces, like the best-selling No Name, vanilla soft serve rolled in pretzels and dipped in chocolate, then laid in a boat and topped with sea salt and lots of caramel (insider tip: go wild and ask to add buckeyes and/or cookie dough as well). Gail's personal go-to among the hard serve flavors is Cappuccino Crunch, a coffee-based ice cream with fudge and Heath (an underrated candy, she says). On the soft serve side, her favorite is the Peanut Butter Piggy, vanilla soft serve in a waffle cone rolled in Muddy Buddies and cookie dough pieces, again laid in a boat and topped with hot fudge and peanut butter sauces. These creations invite you to start with a spoon and end with

King Kone's sweetly smiling sprinkled queen approves of a classic cone. *Navatsyk Photography.*

the cone, or vice versa, for the best of both worlds.

Well versed in King Kone's rich history as part of the local community, the Hewitts took over knowing it was as much about memories as it was the menu. "We wanted a place that people would come to on dates, they would bring their grandparents and grandchildren, their families, their friends, and everyone in between," says Gail. "We wanted it to be that place that when people visit home, they have to stop. And when

It all starts with the perfect twist of soft serve at King Kone. *Navatsyk Photography.*

people move away, they talk about that little place they used to go to get ice cream."

Furthering the community feel, King Kone partners with D is for Delicious homemade chocolate chip cookies and Maggie's Doughnuts and uses homemade cinnamon rolls baked by a local woman. They also host a yearly Kids Day at the Kone, where they offer free kids' cones alongside face painting, balloon artistry and superhero visits while collecting tips for a local charity.

"Chardon as a community has always been special. It is a place where people come together to support one another. If you have a need, people will meet it," Gail says. "There are moments at King Kone where I look around, hear the music playing with the twinkle lights on, and I'll see a dad dancing with his little girl, a couple snuggled together whispering, kids sitting in the beds of their trucks, and everyone is eating our ice cream. It's America at its finest. Freedom, fun, laughter, relationships, community, people. It's about so much more than the food." With a tagline of "May All Your Memories Be Sweet," King Kone delivers on both.

PETE'S ICE CREAM

https://www.petesicecream.com/

Born and raised in Lima, Ohio, Dave Peters recalls the history of the area as "a heavy industrial region yet surrounded by farm country." Growing up, Dave visited the then-popular Eldora Dairy on Cable Road, where local kids could sit on stools and watch through the glass as the cows were milked, then taste the results of this hard work being turned into ice cream right on-site.

This memory, alongside a history of family businesses, inspired Dave to open Pete's Ice Cream in 2009. "My parents both owned businesses growing up and I had sold another business I had owned for 20 years and was looking for something I could get passionate about," he says. "I chose the location [formerly the Dixie Dairy Stand] because it was the first Ice

Cream Stand in our county and had been closed for 10 years. I had a blank canvas and no old reputations to try and undo." With only a reputation to build, Dave set his sights on quality, both on the hand dip and soft serve sides of the operation.

First, for the hand dip, Pete's offers forty flavors, ranging from nostalgic classics like green mint chip to Cappuccino Crunch, which Dave says has "a rich coffee and fudge taste with toffee pieces that are sure to please. And I don't even like coffee." But his go-to is a simpler summer staple from the other side of things, the ever-eternal, smile-inducing soft serve in vanilla or chocolate. Soft serve is also uniquely used in Pete's ice cream sandwiches, swirled super high between two chocolate wafer cookies. Special promotions add meaningful color to the ice cream offerings, such as days dedicated to autism awareness (blue ice cream), Alzheimer's awareness (purple ice cream) and St. Patrick's Day (green ice cream).

Shakes and sundaes, floats and malts, plus a blended offering dubbed an Avalanche round out the offerings on the sweet side, alongside seasonal specials, such as apple dumplings, with or without ice cream (but obviously with). To offset the sweet, a savory side of the menu offers snacks like walking tacos and sandwiches—such as sloppy joes or Italian sausage—but it's under Specialty Dogs Sauces that you'll find the Pete Dog: a combination of bacon, cheese, tomato and mayo to top your regular or footlong hot dog.

Made locally in 2009, Pete's neon lights up the night, leading Lima to indulge. *Dave Peters.*

Quickly gaining a loyal following—including being voted number one in best of the region voting—the new standard for ice cream in Allen County needed to expand, purchasing additional property next to the stand and opening a drive-thru in 2012, just three years into the business. According to Dave, it was "the best move I could have made," helping maintain operations during the 2020 and 2021 seasons through the COVID-19 pandemic.

Ingenuity and hard work are core to Lima, Dave Peters and Pete's Ice Cream. "Our German, Irish and Italian heritage [as a community] lend itself to hardworking folks with appetites to match, and ice cream is a big seller," says Dave. "We have many great

Revived by the roadside, Pete's is bringing new life to Lima's ice cream scene. *Dave Peters.*

ice cream businesses in the Northwest Sector. The main reason I admire some of these great places is their longevity and history." Pete's Ice Cream is on its way to joining their ranks well into the future.

Inside Scoop: Cones, Coneys and Cars, Oh My!

Dave is a vintage car lover, and accordingly, Pete's offers a "Classic Car Discount": 10 percent off your order anytime you come in with your vintage vehicle. Cruise on in and enjoy some great food and ice cream.

Chapter 5

THE FUTURE OF FROZEN

Showing no signs of slowing down when it comes to trends in frozen treats, Ohio continues to be a most fertile field for entrepreneurs in the ice cream industry. First, the mobile food scene has embraced the frozen form, harkening full circle to the good ole Good Humor days and giving both Little Ladies Soft Serve and Mark's Homemade Ice Cream their start. Next, international inspiration has introduced an entirely new format, transforming the scoop or swirl into the eye-catching creations of Simply Rolled. And leveraging social media, independent purveyors, such as Indulgence Ice Cream and Charlotte & Olivia's, sell direct to consumer, skipping the storefront entirely.

Ice cream is a canvas, equal parts classic and creative, and the industry is always encouraging innovators to continue the quest for fresh ideas in the frozen space. Quick to build a fan base, these future-thinking business builders are looking ahead and carrying the state's long legacy forward in the tastiest ways imaginable.

LITTLE LADIES SOFT SERVE

https://www.littleladiessoftserve.com/

It all started with an old postal service truck. In the summer of 2017, Lydia and Will Chambers, having relocated from Philadelphia, Pennsylvania, to

The Little Ladies Soft
Serve truck roaming
the hungry streets of
Columbus. *Phil Navatsyk.*

Columbus a few years prior, were in search of an opportunity that would allow Lydia to balance work with raising their two (now three) young daughters. Inspired by her sister and brother-in-law, Gail and Mitch Hewitt, who already owned King Kone, an ice cream shop and truck in northeast Ohio (Chardon), Lydia put her faith in her culinary background and Will's carpentry skills (one of his life's mottos is "DIY or die") and secured the truck, sight unseen, in an online auction.

While Will spent the following winter and spring converting the blank canvas into an absolutely adorable ice cream truck, Lydia worked on the menu, starting with super soft serve. High-end ice cream bases in vanilla and chocolate serve as the foundation, with the two combining in an iconic swirl. Though the base in and of itself is definitely delicious, the real fun starts with Lydia's toppings, kitschy combinations of ingredients ranging from store-bought cereals to homemade sauces, crumbles and midwestern treats like "puppy chow" (cereal mixed with melted chocolate, peanut butter and powdered sugar).

Giving fun, old-timey names to menu staples and seasonal specials, the couple first paid homage to their eldest daughter, Mabel, after which the operation's signature sprinkle cone is named. Little Ladies' Sparkle Sprinkles, a fanciful take on the topping, are made special with edible gold dust. Second-born Ida's namesake is a sundae (also available as a cone) gone wild with Fruity Pebbles, white chocolate crumble, a strawberry cookie stick and marshmallow sauce. Ohio's iconic peanut butter and chocolate combination, the buckeye, makes its appearance in mini form on the best-selling Aggie, which also boasts a double down of hot fudge and peanut butter sauce as well as the aforementioned puppy chow. Lydia's favorite? The Luella, her take on another summer staple, the s'more, with a classic roasted marshmallow, amped-up brown butter graham cracker crumble and upgraded chocolate in the form of Nutella. Monthly truck specials rotate based on seasonal produce and have included flavor profiles like raspberry lemon, key lime and peach cobbler.

After two successful seasons developing a loyal following, Lydia and Will welcomed a third "little lady," daughter Flannery, as well as Lydia's brother Phil Navatsyk and his wife, Courtny, which timed out perfectly. The younger couple had taken time off to travel after Courtny's contract as a news reporter ended, and they returned to look for work just before the COVID-19 pandemic began. "I've always had strong intuition," recalls Lydia, "and I just knew they needed to run [the truck]." They stepped up to the challenge as food trucks began booking individual neighborhoods while events were cancelled, and afternoon and evening time slots filled up quickly; the truck was booked during both most days.

As they were an expanding family operation, a brick-and-mortar location felt both feasible and necessary to sustain the positive momentum. While Lydia was willing to entertain a full build-out, Will's practicality won her over, leading them to select a spot in Westerville that needed less of

Meet the Luella, a Little Ladies twist on the classic s'more, upgraded with Nutella. *Phil Navatsyk.*

Little Ladies Soft Serve, now also in brick and mortar. *Phil Navatsyk.*

an overhaul, one mainly focused on equipment and aesthetics. Opened in the fall of 2021, the shop offers what were previously seasonal sundaes permanently, such as fan favorites like the Bernadette (a combination of homemade brownie chunks, potato chips, hot fudge sauce and Florin coffee) and the Ruby (which features strawberry sauce, candied pretzels, strawberry shortcake crumble, strawberry compote, whipped cream and a cherry), as well as Flannery's featured flavor (bananas foster bread pudding, corn puff brittle and a maple bourbon caramel). Another fun shop-only addition are Sundae Flights: mini versions of menu items, allowing visitors to try a few at a time, as truck visitors always have a hard time choosing.

The family divides responsibilities, with Lydia handling most of the work behind the scenes, including booking events and email communications, while Phil and Courtny handle social media posts and serve customers, both on the truck and at the shop. And the truck isn't going anywhere; it's back for private events during the "season." But while it takes the winter off, the shop can still offer new seasonal sundaes, including holiday-themed ones; Lydia's excited about exploring flavor profiles she hasn't yet been able to. With a close-knit family behind it and exciting combinations yet to be tapped, there's little doubt this originally mobile ice cream business will stay on a roll well into the future.

Mark's Homemade Ice Cream

https://www.markshomemadeicecream.com/

Starting a business while still in college isn't for the faint of heart. But Mark Pfeifer had been preparing for this undertaking for quite literally his whole life—from his first tiny taste of mint chocolate chip snuck from a family friend at the age of just seven months, to a high school report written on his future goal of opening an ice cream shop. So, why wait any longer? When the opportunity arose in 2016, while Mark was just a sophomore at the University of Akron, to purchase both an ice cream batch freezer and, subsequently, an equipment truck the local fire department in his hometown of Bucyrus was retiring, he took the leap.

Supported by his entire family—his parents, Ed and Jenny Lynne; his sisters, Lydia and Lindsey (and Lindsey's husband, Jordan, at whose 2016 wedding Mark gained an early following) and his then-girlfriend, now-wife, Allison—Mark's Homemade Ice Cream hit the streets in May 2017. Having perfected his core recipes (getting just the right flavor for his chocolate was particularly tricky) and fully remodeling the old fire equipment truck (except for its top lights and "Emergency Call 911" tribute to its past) alongside his dad and uncle, Mark spent the season busily crossing town to bring his irresistibly creamy concoctions to celebrations: from graduation parties and weddings to festivals and events at corporations and clubs. When he wasn't fully booked, he gained a following outside of the local Family Video—one

Two scoops at Mark's Homemade. *Mark's Homemade Ice Cream.*

big enough that for the 2018 season, another truck was added to the fleet, this one a former construction equipment hauler, originally bright yellow, now painted to match its sister's signature red and named Norton for her former hometown.

At the center of this great growth trajectory is Mark's high-quality product, which he still makes himself, just six gallons at a time. The batch freezer allows him to add a wide variety of ingredients, from whole Oreos for his cookies and cream (both Ed's and Jenny Lynne's favorite flavor) to pie filling for the seasonal apple pie flavor. Peanut butter is another family favorite, shared by Mark himself, as well as Lydia and Jordan, while Allison loves seasonal strawberry but is also working on convincing Mark to make a grape.

Just five years into operating the mobile units, Mark took another leap, bringing new life to the shuttered Daily Scoop building in the north end of downtown Bucyrus, across from another local favorite, Baker's Pizza Sports Shack. A drive-thru, outdoor seating and "Shop Specials" all draw customers to this brick-and-mortar outpost, including Mark's menu favorite, the brownie sundae (a thick, homemade brownie, warmed and topped with a scoop of vanilla ice cream, chocolate sauce and whipped cream and cherry) alongside a Tin Roof Sundae (vanilla ice cream topped with chocolate sauce, Spanish peanuts, whipped cream and a cherry) and a root beer float. Milkshakes and make-your-own sundaes round out the menu, as well as pup cups for four-legged companions and junior scoops for the littlest ice cream lovers (or the indecisive—the Sampler features four junior scoops).

Having grown up on a four-generation dairy farm, Mark has the business in his blood, understanding the "joy and hard work of caring for over 500 animals 365 days a year and striving for the highest quality product possible." As a nod to this lineage, he's been given a few glass milk bottles with his great-great-grandfather's name etched on them from the time when he was a dairy farmer and local milkman. Being able to continue this legacy in a new format still in his hometown brings Mark pride. "Bucyrus is a rural town with a lot of history. We just celebrated our bicentennial this summer." He adds, "Opening a scoop shop in my hometown has been the businesses' success to date. Ice cream in my opinion is the best part of dairying."

While future operations are rooted in the area (Mark transitioned from renting production space to his own facility, also in 2021), business growth is targeted on expansion across Ohio via pints available in grocery stores and restaurants (some smaller central Ohio outlets have already begun carrying pints year-round). Mark is fueled by the success of his competition, saying of these plans, "Our area is the perfect spot for my business to get started and grow. To our north is Toft's, and to the south is Graeter's, Jeni's, and all of the great Columbus area ice cream. Mitchell's in Cleveland was a big inspiration for me. The way they make their ice cream (by the batch) inspires me to think that I too could grow to a size similar to them, even by making small batch ice cream. And their product is excellent."

Mark sees the industry as a whole on a similar trajectory to one you might not typically compare with ice cream: craft beer. But the parallel makes sense when he expands, saying, "I believe people will turn to the more local, premium products in the future. Less quantity, more quality." He continues,

"In the industry overall, I see continued growth in premium, artisan brands. We have opened in an area without a dominant ice cream brand, giving us a chance to grow and succeed."

Inside Scoop: Brake for Brats in Bucyrus

Bucyrus is known as the Bratwurst Capital of America and has been holding an annual Bratwurst Festival each summer since 1968.

Simply Rolled

https://www.simplyrolledicecream.com/

Ice cream has long been appealing to multiple senses: first the eyes, then the taste buds. But in 2009, a new trend took over Thailand and turned the look of ice cream as we knew it on its head, giving it even more visual appeal. Quickly spreading across social media channels, rolled ice cream, as it's called, hit the East Coast of the United States by 2015. Inspired by a trip to Thailand, Shannon Sano brought the creation to Columbus in 2016, opening Simply Rolled as a pop-up shop inside of a neighborhood grocer, then eventually taking over the space entirely in 2017.

The process is as eye-catching as the product. A liquid ice cream base is poured onto an ice pan, an extremely cold metal circle, then moved across the surface, first spread thinly, then rolled into strips. Every order is distinct; customers choose their ingredients, then watch the rolls being created and topped. "It's not only the freshest ice cream you'll ever eat, but it's fun to watch as well," says Shannon.

Signature offerings range from Salty Caramel Pretzel and Gone Bananas to an ode to rolled ice cream's Asian roots in the Matcha Berry. House-made buckeye candies and edible cookie dough (also available standalone, with toppings) are the stars of Buckeye Madness and Cookie Dough Boy, respectively, while create-your-own creations can start with anything from Coconut Ash (sweet coconut cream colored black by activated charcoal) to Thai Tea, Birthday Cake and Cotton Candy. Shannon's custom order? "Vegan Dark Chocolate!" she exclaims. "It's a perfect blend of pure cocoa, cashew, and coconut cream and is the creamiest vegan ice cream around. It's delicious when paired with bananas and peanut butter sauce."

Additions like homemade Buckeyes and Edible Cookie Dough top off the distinctly different ice cream offering of Simply Rolled. *Simply Rolled Ice Cream.*

Seasonal features range from energetic combinations like Java Mocha Chip to a fresh take on Pumpkin Pie Roll, made with an actual slice of pumpkin pie rolled in. And then there's the year-round Cotton Candy Burrito. "It's definitely a fan favorite and the most unique offering on our menu," says Shannon. "It consists of cotton candy ice cream with sprinkles, marshmallow sauce, Fruity Pebbles, and mini marshmallows, all rolled into a burrito wrap made of cotton candy!" Talk about a foodie fusion, huh?

The concept was received so well in Columbus that 2018 saw early expansion to Cincinnati, with a second location in Over the Rhine (now under franchise ownership). "Both of our current stores are in areas that are vibrant, welcoming communities. On any given day, you will see people, young and old, walking the sidewalks and enjoying the many different restaurants, boutiques, and art galleries in the area," notes Shannon, with a nod to the origins of the business and wanting to keep the concept "as close to its roots as possible, we chose areas that have a sense of community and creativity." Creative and craveable, trendy and tasty, Simply Rolled is stunningly delicious.

INDULGENCE ICE CREAM

Social @indulgenceicecream

With names like Shock the Monkey, Mad About Saffron and CRACK!, it's no wonder Dan Rhule's side gig making ice cream is fun—and a bit indulgent—both for him and his customers. Dan started making ice cream professionally (a term he says he uses "as loosely as possible") as a word-of-mouth-based home business in 2015, with a direct-to-consumer model and a few local restaurant partners.

One of those restaurant partners, La Tavola in Grandview, had recently opened when Dan went in for a dinner he now recalls as a "turning point." Since he had some experience working with another (now closed) restaurant in New Albany, his ears perked up when the La Tavola server mentioned that everything was made in-house. "Even your gelato?" asked Dan, to which the server replied, "Actually, that's the only thing that isn't." Taking the opportunity to slide him a business card, Dan replied, "How would you like to have it made in-house?" His card made its way to owner and chef Rick Lopez, who asked for a meeting and, after tasting Dan's samples, began a relationship that's expanded, as Lopez has opened Lupo in neighboring Upper Arlington, offering flavors like Horchata and Olive Oil Orange Zest. This partnership, as well as others, including ones with Pretentious Barrel House, Spagio, Aubergine, the Kitchen and Basic Biscuits, has given Dan a unique perspective on the local food scene. "I think most people outside of the area are surprised to see how strong the culinary scene is here in Columbus. We have a lot of incredible restaurants and food stores," he says. "The competition is tough and it's a challenge to continue to operate at a high level and also try to be innovative."

This focus on innovation comes through in Dan's distinctive offering, a consistently rotating lineup with names as fun as their flavors. Best sellers include Caramel Brownie Cheesecake, Peanut Obsession and BuckeyeScream, as well as the aforementioned Mad About Saffron (a saffron and pistachio ice cream), Shock the Monkey (a cinnamon cream cheese ice cream with chunks of monkey bread) and CRACK! (a brown sugar ice cream with chunks of cracker toffee). Breakfast-inspired Coffee and

The Indulgence Ice Cream crew smiling in shirts that say it all. *Dan Rhule.*

Dan scooping at a La Tavola pop-up event. *Dan Rhule.*

Donuts and Cereal Killer (cereal milk ice cream) are crowd pleasers, along with cinematic references, such as Movie Night (a buttered popcorn flavor with chopped dark chocolate, peanuts and a caramel swirl) and the Dude (a boozy white Russian ice cream). Dan's personal go-to is his Belgian Bliss (a cookie butter ice cream with chopped spiced cookies and dark chocolate), which also happens to be the one that got him started with restaurant customers.

Inspired originally by both local and national ice cream makers, Dan lists Jeni's ("the Queen on the block"), Graeter's (with a very loyal following), Johnson's, CRMD and Handel's among the amazing ice creams in Columbus, alongside Salt & Straw in Portland, Oregon, also known for its inventive flavors. "But, really, I respect all of them because I know how hard they all work and how difficult it is to just survive in the food industry, let alone be successful," he adds, acknowledging that "as a 1-person operation, I have the freedom to try unique things and use original flavor names and I have the safety net of not relying on the sales of ice cream for financial security. So, I admire and respect those people who are working hard to pay not only their own bills, but to offer employment opportunities for others."

With no storefront, Dan arranges pickups via social media channels and personally hand delivers his products. While some might see this as an extra burden, Dan finds the interaction to be a perk, saying, "This little hobby of mine provides emotional feedback that I don't get in my 'real' job." He adds, "No one has ever come up to me and said 'Dan, that report you wrote, that was AMAZING!' But I sometimes get that feedback in the ice cream world and that's why I do this."

Dan's passion for ice cream comes through in his hobby turned side gig, and customers rave over the smooth, creamy texture of his small-batch creations. He plans to maintain his current business model for the near future, while participating in occasional pop-up events with friends in related food businesses, including collaborations with Bakes by Lo, Lion Cub Cookies and the Buckeye Lady. "My biggest challenge is time," he says, "until I am able to retire from my full time job, then I'll decide if I want to open a storefront, continue in the current mode, or just enjoy retirement." Until then, he'll continue to innovate, as he sees the category as a whole trending toward new and unusual flavor combinations, and fans can continue to get their fix of Dan's latest creations while they hold out hope for his future plans.

CHARLOTTE & OLIVIA'S

https://www.charlotteandolivias.com/

Another cottage ice cream business has an equally loyal following just across town, with a seasonal presence at the New Albany Farmers Market and year-round doorstep delivery. Started in 2011 by Jim Cushing, Charlotte & Olivia's Sublime Ice Creams is a labor of love that got its seed when Jim himself was just a boy, spending summers shucking corn and cranking ice cream. "I make the ice cream the same way my mom did when I was a kid," says Jim, originally from Lancaster, Ohio. The taste memory is still with him, as he adds, "I loved the ice cream my mom made. It was so simple and pure—fresh and frosty. It's the inspiration for all the ice creams we make."

But it was Jim's friends who pushed him to start selling his ice cream after the company he had been working for lost its contract. Seeing the situation as an opportunity, he remembers thinking, "If not now, when?" Ten years later, sales have climbed consistently year after year, with success rooted in the high-quality product. Jim rents commercial space part time to make his ice cream, using only Ohio dairy, pure cane sugar and as many local ingredients as possible. None of his ice creams use anything artificial, nor do they contain any preservatives or stabilizers. "Our ice cream actually melts," Jim says. "Isn't ice cream supposed to melt?"

This purity allows the flavors to really stand out, and with bold profiles like Caffeine, Chocolate Sin, Fleur de Sel and Caramel and Fresh Mint with Chocolate, Jim doesn't hold back. His personal favorites change with the seasons, with summer bringing Strawberry Meringue and fall's football-focused Buckeye Proud, billed as "a new Central Ohio tradition." Many of these fan favorites feature partnerships with other local businesses, including coffee from Backroom Coffee Roasters, peanut butter from Shell Dust, lemon liquor from Tessora and produce including honey from farms like Lastshaw Honey, Dorans Farm and Wishwell.

Speaking of central Ohio, Jim nods to both the city of Columbus and its surrounding suburbs as "diverse with an amazing foodie culture."

Charlotte & Olivia's homespun take on Madagascar Vanilla Bean is pure and simple. *Jim Cushing.*

In case of emergency, Charlotte & Olivia's delivers an especially sublime dose of calcium. *Jim Cushing.*

Specifically in New Albany, where he makes his ice cream and whose residents make up the largest group of his fan base, "It's an upscale rural lifestyle that celebrates community and family, art and architecture, health and wellness, local matters as well as a world view." And he believes in supporting the community that supports him, with a portion of every sale going to further the mission of local charities, such as Healthy New Albany, the New Albany Community Foundation, the New Albany Farmers Market, New Albany Food Pantry and the Mid-Ohio Food Bank.

This sense of culinary openness and acceptance is evident in the restaurant scene as well as for artisanally made products like ice cream. "Columbus is the home of Jeni's, and if it wasn't for that business I would never have gained my own following," Jim says. "Her ice cream is known for local ingredients, unusual flavors and a higher price point. Following in those footsteps made it easier for us to produce a quality product at a higher price than what else was available at the time." He also admires smaller producers as well: "All the small guys out there making quality ice cream from real ingredients. They don't strive to be the biggest, just to offer the best." Likewise, Jim's focus remains local: "I don't have huge aspirations to be the next big thing, I just like making beautiful ice cream and sharing it with my customers. We don't need to be Ben & Jerry's, just Charlotte & Olivia's."

HONORABLE MENTIONS

Ohio today may very well have as many (if not more) ice cream shops as it once did dairies—far too many to detail in the space of one book. The sampling here pays homage to Ohio's past, present and future in the stories of the familial and individual entrepreneurs who have capitalized on the state's rich farming heritage to bring its people the tastiest (at least in this author's humble midwestern opinion) frozen treats in the country.

While time, space and other constraints may have prevented including the following shops, their loyalist followings indicated they, at minimum, deserve a mention, in case readers still have room for just one more scoop after touring the shops profiled in more depth. As it would be impossible for even this list to be exhaustive, the conversation continues on this author's social media channels @rcasteelcook—send me your scoop!

The dairy deliciousness continues at:

Almost Heaven Homemade Ice Cream
Big Ed's
Bird's Sweets and Treats
Bold Face Dairy Bar
Buckeye Country Creamery
Buona Terra
Cathy's Gourmet Ice Cream Sandwiches
Charlotte's Ice Cream (Willoughby)
Cherry Street Creamery
Churn Gourmet Handcrafted
City Sweets & Creamery
Cockeye Creamery
Connie's Affogato
Coolspot Country Market
Cowboy Cones
Cruisin' Coneheads

Dairy Corner
Dari De-lite
Davis Cookie Collection
Deersville General Store
Dojo Gelato
Durbin Magic Freeze
Eishaus
Emma's Frosty Kreme
Eric's Ice Cream Factory
Flub's Dair-ette
General Custer's Golf and Gulp
Golden Gelato
Gold Top Dairy Bar
Granny's Goodies on the Go
Green Man Twist
Heavenly Creamery
Hello Honey
Hometown Swirls
Jubie's Creamery
Katie's Korner
Kirke's Homemade Ice Cream
Knueven Creamery & Market
La Grassa
Lil e's Ice Cream
Lil' Goodie Shoppe
Loveland Dairy Whip
Ludlow Parlor
M&T's Twisted Treats
Michael's Ice Cream
Milk Jar Café
Miller's Creamery
Miller's Drive-In
Mootown Creamery
Mr. Freeze
Mt. Healthy Dairy Bar
Mt. Washington Creamy Whip

Norwood Delite Creamy Whip
Nuhfer Premium Ice Cream
Old Man's Cave General Store
Old Milford Parlor
Pav's Creamery
Pendleton Parlor
Piper's Cafe
Roll n Go
Round Hill Dairy
Schneider's Sweet Shop
Silver Grove Dari-Bar
Sprinkles Creamy Whip
Stoner's Ice Cream Parlor
Strickland's Frozen Custard
Swaffy's Ice Cream
Sweet Tooth Ice Cream Truck
Terry Family Ice Cream Shoppe
Terry's Ice Cream Dairy Bar
The Cone Zone
The Dip
The Dipper
The Golden Bear
The Goody Shop
The Ice Box Dairy Bar
The Ice Cream Rollery
The Root Beer Stand
The Twist
Town Trolley
Tucker's Whippy Dip
Twist Ice Cream Company
United Dairy Farmers (UDF)
Walker Bros. Ice Cream
Weldon's Ice Cream Factory
Whip-n-Dip
Z's Cream & Bean

BIBLIOGRAPHY

Articles

Crowl, Thomas E. "From Copper Kettle to Klondikes: The Isaly's Story." *Timeline* (a publication of the Ohio History Connection) 21, no. 2 (March/April 2004): 26–41.

Books

Damerow, Gail. *Ice Cream! The Whole Scoop*. Lakewood, CO: Glenbridge, 1996.

Dickson, Paul. *The Great American Ice Cream Book*. New York: Atheneum, 1978.

Funderburg, Anne Cooper. *Chocolate, Strawberry, and Vanilla: A History of American Ice Cream*. Bowling Green, OH: Bowling Green State University Popular Press, 1995.

Visser, Margaret. *Much Depends on Dinner*. New York: Grove, 1986.

Websites

About Staff. "Eureka! | Mid-1800s." July 30, 2014. https://www.aboutstark.com/features/eureka-mid-1800s/.

Adolphus, David Traver. "Ding-a-ling-a-ling! Must be the Good Humor Man!" *Hemmings Motor News*, January 2010. https://www.hemmings.com/stories/article/ding-a-ling-a-ling.

Anchor Hocking. "Vintage Fountainware Footed Glass Sherbet Dish, 4.5 Ounces." Accessed December 2, 2021. https://www.anchorhocking.com/anchor-hocking-glass-footed-sherbet-dish-4-5-ounce.html.

———. "Vintage Fountainware Glass Banana Split Dish, 8.25 Inches." Accessed December 2, 2021. https://www.anchorhocking.com/anchor-hocking-glass-banana-split-dish-8-25-inches.html.

Ashland County Historical Society. "Looking Back at…Ashland Sanitary Dairy." Accessed December 2, 2021. https://ashlandhistory.org/lookingback.html.

Banana Split Festival Facebook page. "Banana Split Festival Added a New… Banana Split Festival." https://www.facebook.com/thebananasplitfestival/photos/pcb.2368290963214348/2368290763214368.

Bell, Don. "History of Ice Cream—Discover the Amazing Facts and Folklore." Homemade Dessert Recipes. Accessed December 2, 2021. https://www.homemade-dessert-recipes.com/history-of-ice-cream.html.

Berkes, Anna. "Ice Cream | Thomas Jefferson's Monticello." Monticello.org. https://www.monticello.org/site/research-and-collections/ice-cream.

Busbey, Tim. "Miller's Hawkins Market Celebrates Grand Opening in Ashland." Richland Source. July 31, 2017. https://www.richlandsource.com/ashland_source/millers-hawkins-market-celebrates-grand-opening-in-ashland/article_1e40e53e-7623-11e7-a132-835662f0266d.html.

Butler, Suzanne. "Erlenbusch, 'Purity' Ice Cream." *German Village News*, March 2015. https://germanvillage.com/wp-content/uploads//2015/03/Erlenbusch.pdf.

Cain, Brenda. "Akron Brothers Invented the Ice Cream Cone; Descendants Keep the Legacy Alive (Video)." Cleveland.com. August 24, 2016. https://www.cleveland.com/best/2016/08/akron_brothers_invented_the_ic.html.

Carlson, Brady. "The Great Banana Split Rivalry (Cool Weird Awesome 57)." June 7, 2019. https://www.bradycarlson.com/the-great-banana-split-rivalry/.

Carosa, Chris. "Hamburger WhoDunIt Part V: CSI: Hamburg(Er), N.Y." September 5, 2018. https://chriscarosa.com/2018/09/hamburger-whodunit-part-v-csi-hamburger-n-y/.

Cho, Janet H. "Pierre's Ice Cream Opens New $9.2 Million Production Facility in Cleveland." *Plain Dealer* (Cleveland, CO), June 14, 2011. https://www.cleveland.com/business/2011/06/pierres_ice_cream_opens_new_92_million_production_facility_in_cleveland.html.

Cincinnati CityBeat. "17 Essential Cincinnati Creamy Whips You Need to Visit This Summer." May 29, 2020. https://photos.citybeat.com/19-essential-cincinnati-creamy-whips-you-need-to-visit-this-summer/?slide=1&annman_zipdip_jf.

Cleveland Scene. "Best Blast from the Past 2003." Accessed December 2, 2021. https://www.clevescene.com/cleveland/best-blast-from-the-past/BestOf?oid=1535646.

Columbus Neighborhoods. "Beechwold/Wittich's Soda Fountain." April 20, 2017. https://columbusneighborhoods.org/video/beechwoldwittichs-soda-fountain/.

———. "From the Vault: Erlenbusch Ice Cream Shop." December 6, 2017. https://columbusneighborhoods.org/video/from-the-vault-erlenbusch-ice-cream-shop/.

Conradt, Stacy. "Who Really Invented the Ice Cream Soda?" Mental Floss. June 18, 2015. https://www.mentalfloss.com/article/64970/who-really-invented-ice-cream-soda.

Culgan, Rossilynne. "Unwrapping the Klondike Bar's History in Pittsburgh." *York Daily Record*, May 19, 2018. https://www.ydr.com/story/life/2018/05/19/unwrapping-klondike-bars-history-pittsburgh/625843002/.

Dager, Luconda. "Secrets from a 105-Year-Old Ice Cream Company." Dairy Foods. December 3, 2018. https://www.dairyfoods.com/blogs/14-dairy-foods-blog/post/93295-secrets-from-a-105-year-old-ice-cream-company.

DeMuth, Baylee. "Wittich's Candy Shop, Circleville." *Ohio Magazine*, August 2019. https://www.ohiomagazine.com/food-drink/article/wittich-s-candy-shop-circleville.

EricT_CulinaryLore. "Where Did 'I Scream, You Scream, We All Scream for Ice Cream' Come From?" March 5, 2014. https://culinarylore.com/food-history:i-scream-you-scream-ice-cream/.

Eschner, Kat. "The Weird, Brief History of the Eskimo Pie Corporation." *Smithsonian*, January 24, 2017. https://www.smithsonianmag.com/smart-news/weird-short-history-eskimo-pie-corporation-180961840/.

Evans, Farrell. "Why Ice Cream Soared in Popularity During Prohibition." HISTORY. Accessed December 2, 2021. https://www.history.com/news/ice-cream-boom-1920s-prohibition.

Farmers' Almanac Staff. "Happy National Ice Cream Day! Where Did Ice Cream Come From?" *Farmers' Almanac*, June 29, 2010. https://www.farmersalmanac.com/where-did-ice-cream-come-from-2-11190.

50States.com. "Ohio Facts and Trivia." 2019. https://www.50states.com/facts/ohio.htm.

Good Humor. "100 Years of Good Humor." https://www.goodhumor.com/us/en/our-history.html.

———. "Our Products." https://www.goodhumor.com/us/en/products.html.

GreenAcres Market. "After All These Years, We're Still Screaming for Ice Cream." July 6, 2017. https://greenacres.com/years-still-screaming-ice-cream/.

Hamper, Anietra. "Wilmington: Home of the Banana Split." *Ohio Magazine*, August 10, 2018. https://ohio.org/wps/portal/gov/tourism/travel-inspiration/articles/wilmington-home-of-the-banana-split.

Havenner, Nathan. "Birthplace of the Banana Split." *Ohio Magazine*, June 2017. https://www.ohiomagazine.com/food-drink/article/birthplace-of-the-banana-split.

Hechmer, Rita. "Ohio's Best Ice Cream 2021." Ohio Farm Bureau. July 23, 2021. https://ofbf.org/2021/07/23/ohios-best-ice-cream-2021/.

Honky Tonk Foodie. "Historical Ice Cream Molds Now Unique Collector's Items." Texas Hill Country. November 12, 2020. https://texashillcountry.com/ice-cream-molds-collectors-items/.

How Products Are Made. "How Ice Cream Is Made—Production Process, Making, History, Used, Product, Industry, Machine, History." 2014. http://www.madehow.com/Volume-3/Ice-Cream.html.

Ice Screamers. "Who Invented the Ice Cream Cone?" 2020. https://www.icescreamers.com/NewsletterArticle.html.

International Dairy Foods Association. "The History of the Ice Cream Cone." https://www.idfa.org/the-history-of-the-ice-cream-cone.

Jeffries, Anna. "Utica Sertoma Ice Cream Festival Hits 40." Newark Advocate. May 21, 2014. https://www.newarkadvocate.com/story/news/2014/05/21/utica-sertoma-ice-cream-festival-hits-40/9344709/.

KaleidoScoops. "The History of Ice Cream Machines." 2017. https://www.kalscoops.com/history-ice-cream-machines/.

Kaple, Lori Adams. "Ashland Sanitary Dairy—A Successful Business and Popular Hangout." Ashland Source. August 17, 2019. https://www.ashlandsource.com/history/ashland-sanitary-dairy-a-successful-business-and-popular-hangout/article_f4125398-c034-11e9-b09e-cb677cfe8e19.html.

Mahoning Valley Historical Society. "History of the Burt Confectionery & Creation of the 'Good Humor' Bar." August 3, 2012. https://mahoninghistory.org/tyler-history-center/the-good-humor-story/.

McCosham, Sarah. "Ultimate Guide to Cincinnati Creamy Whip Stands." *Southwest Ohio Parent Magazine*, March 10, 2020. https://ohparent.com/ultimate-guide-to-cincinnati-creamy-whip-stands/.

Melito, Steve. "January 29, 1924—The Ice Cream Cone Rolling Machine." Engineering360. January 29, 2009. https://cr4.globalspec.com/blogentry/8017/January-29-1924-The-Ice-Cream-Cone-Rolling-Machine.

Menches Bros. "Menches Brothers—Inventors of the Hamburger—Northeast Ohio." Accessed December 2, 2021. https://www.menchesbros.com/.

Moak, Jefferson. "The Frozen Sucker War: Good Humor v. Popsicle." *Prologue Magazine* 37, no. 1 (Spring 2005). https://www.archives.gov/publications/prologue/2005/spring/popsicle-1.html.

Nibble. "The History of the Ice Cream Freezer." https://www.thenibble.com/reviews/main/ice-cream/the-history-of-ice-cream3.asp.

O'Connor, Patrick. "Debate on Ice-Cream Cone's Origins Rages Hot and Cold." *Chicago Tribune*, April 15, 2004. https://www.chicagotribune.com/news/ct-xpm-2004-04-15-0404150073-story.html.

Ohio Farm Bureau. "Vote for Ohio's BEST Ice Cream!" Accessed December 2, 2021. https://ofbf.app.do/polls/ohio-ice-cream-battle-2021/forms/closed.

Ohio History Central. "Banana Split." Accessed December 2, 2021. https://ohiohistorycentral.org/w/Banana_Split.

———. "Ice Cream Cone Machine—Ohio History Central." Accessed December 2, 2021. https://ohiohistorycentral.org/w/Ice_Cream_Cone_Machine.

Ohio History Connection. "Search Results" (images of Erlenbusch ice cream molds). Accessed December 2, 2021. http://catalog.ohiohistory.org/Presto/search/ SearchResults. aspx?q=ZXJsZW5idXNjaA%3d%3d&so=eyJTZWFyY2hUZXh0IjoiWlhKsc1pXNWlkWE5q YUE9PSIsIkNvbnRyb2xJZCI6ImFkdlNjcmVlbk NvbnRyb2xJZF8xMDU2NSIsIk9wdGlvbMiOltdfQ%3d%3d.

Ohio State Fair. "Butter Cow." July 4, 2017. https://ohiostatefair.com/traditions/butter-cow/.

Ohio State University. "What Does Ice Cream Have to Do with Ohio State University Extension? | Extension 100." October 13, 2014. https://u.osu.edu/extension100/2014/10/13/what-does-ice-cream-have-to- do-with-ohio-state-university-extension/.

Ohio State University Office of Research. "Perfecting the Drumstick." September 18, 2019. https://research.osu.edu/perfecting-drumstick.

Old World Stone Carving. "Mirror Lake Ice Cream Cone." January 9, 2013. https://www.oldworldstonecarving.com/mirror-lake-ice-cream-cone/.

Pafoodways.omeka.net. "Birthplace of Commercial Ice Cream Production: Pennsylvania Historical Markers: The Land of Penn and Plenty: Bringing History to the Table." https://pafoodways.omeka.net/exhibits/show/pennsylvania-historical-marker/marking-time/birthplace-commercial-icecream.

PBS Food. "Where Is the Best Ice Cream in Ohio?" Accessed December 2, 2021. https://www.pbs.org/food/features/best-ice-cream-ohio/.

Pike, Laurie. "Saying Goodbye to Jim Aglamesis." *Cincinnati Magazine*, May 6, 2021. https://www.cincinnatimagazine.com/article/saying-goodbye-to-jim-aglamesis/.

Preservation Maryland. "Historic Foodways: Making Ice Cream in Maryland." July 16, 2017. https://www.preservationmaryland.org/history-of-ice-cream-in-baltimore-maryland/.

Putz's Creamy Whip. "History." Accessed December 2, 2021. https://www.putzscreamywhip.com/history.

Roaming Hunger. "About the Cone." Accessed December 2, 2021. https://roaminghunger.com/the-cone-cin/.

Sebak, Rick. "The Origins of Isaly's: It's Not What You Think." *Pittsburgh Magazine*, February 15, 2017. https://www.pittsburghmagazine.com/the-origins-of-isalys-its-not-what-you-think/.

Sell, Jill. "Behold, Butter Cow." *Ohio Magazine*, July 2015. https://www.ohiomagazine.com/ohio-life/article/behold-butter-cow.

Severson, Kim. "The American Dreamsicle." *Topic*, June 2017. https://www.topic.com/the-american-dreamsicle.

South High School. "South High School Yearbook 1927." Columbus Metropolitan Library, Columbus Yearbook Collection. https://digital-collections.columbuslibrary.org/digital/collection/yearbook/id/5783/.

Stradley, Linda. "History of Ice Cream Cone." What's Cooking America. May 15, 2015. https://whatscookingamerica.net/History/IceCream/IceCreamCone.htm.

TIME. "Business: Good Humor." September 30, 1935. http://content.time.com/time/subscriber/article/0,33009,749160,00.html.

WCPO. "Aglamesis Ice Cream Patriarch Leaves Legacy of Integrity, Sincerity." January 25, 2021. https://www.wcpo.com/entertainment/local-a-e/longtime-leader-of-aglamesis-ice-cream-and-candy-dies.

WFMJ. "Iconic Ice Cream with Youngstown Roots Celebrates 100 Years." September 10, 2020. https://www.wfmj.com/story/42614565/iconic-ice-cream-with-youngstown-roots-celebrates-100-years.

Wiedrich, Bob. "Drumstick Dons Sundae Best." *Chicago Tribune*, March 7, 1988. https://www.chicagotribune.com/news/ct-xpm-1988-03-07-8804050412-story.html.

Wikipedia. "Anchor Hocking." May 23, 2021. https://en.wikipedia.org/wiki/Anchor_Hocking.

———. "Edy's Pie." Accessed November 12, 2021. https://en.wikipedia.org/wiki/Edy%27s_Pie#cite_note-Duan-4.

———. "Good Humor." Accessed October 30, 2021.https://en.wikipedia.org/wiki/Good_Humor#cite_note-time1-9.

———. "Isaly's." Accessed June 16, 2021. https://en.wikipedia.org/wiki/Isaly%27s.

———. "Pierre's Ice Cream Company." Accessed November 3, 2021. https://en.wikipedia.org/wiki/Pierre%27s_Ice_Cream_Company.

Wiltshire, Cliff. "Unusual Discovery Leads to History Lesson." *Clintonville Spotlight*, August 3, 2018. https://www.clintonvillespotlight.com/articles/unusual-discovery-leads-to-history-lesson/.

Woodiwiss, Bob. "Creamy Whip & Other Delights." *Cincinnati Magazine*, July 1, 2011. https://www.cincinnatimagazine.com/citywiseblog/creamy-whip-other-delights1-2/.

Zeroll. "Our History." Accessed December 2, 2021. https://zeroll.com/pages/about-us.

ABOUT THE AUTHOR

Renee Casteel Cook is a lifelong ice cream lover and recovering advertising industry account executive turned freelance writer, always with a focus on food and beverage. To balance out all of her diligent "research," Renee runs, both for exercise and to keep up with her three lovely little girls, ages six and two (yep, twins!), all in training to enjoy eating equally as much as their mother. Thankfully, Renee not only married into a last name befitting a food writer, but the man who came with it lives up to the title, as her husband, Jim, is the head chef of the house. A Chicago native now based in the heart of the "Heart of It All," Renee embraced the diverse food scene in Columbus through her 2016 title *The Columbus Food Truck Cookbook* and is excited to expand to cities and small towns throughout the state in this guide to Ohio ice cream.